HOW TO READ ULYSSES, AND WHY

PETER LANG
New York • Washington, D.C./Baltimore • Bern
Frankfurt am Main • Berlin • Brussels • Vienna • Oxford

JEFFERSON HUNTER

HOW TO READ *ULYSSES,* AND WHY

PETER LANG
New York • Washington, D.C./Baltimore • Bern
Frankfurt am Main • Berlin • Brussels • Vienna • Oxford

Library of Congress Cataloging-in-Publication Data

Hunter, Jefferson.
How to read "Ulysses," and why / Jefferson Hunter.
p. cm.
Includes bibliographical references (p.).
1. Joyce, James, 1882–1941. Ulysses. I. Title.
PR6019.O9 U6576   823'.912—dc 21   2001038394
ISBN 0-8204-5668-3

Die Deutsche Bibliothek-CIP-Einheitsaufnahme

Hunter, Jefferson:
How to read "Ulysses," and why / Jefferson Hunter.
–New York; Washington, D.C./Baltimore; Bern;
Frankfurt am Main; Berlin; Brussels; Vienna; Oxford: Lang.
ISBN 0-8204-5668-3

Cover design by Lisa Dillon

The paper in this book meets the guidelines for permanence and durability
of the Committee on Production Guidelines for Book Longevity
of the Council of Library Resources.

Printed in the United States of America

To Margaret, Rebecca, and Andrew

Ego sum pauper
Nihil habeo
Cor meum dabo

Acknowledgments

I DO NOT imagine that I am the first to try to explain *Ulysses* but only a figure in a long line, the last term of a preceding series and the first term of a succeeding series, as Joyce wrote about a somewhat different form of human activity. In the preceding series are many authors of books on Joyce, and in the Suggestions for Further Reading I have listed both works to which I think readers of *Ulysses* might profitably turn and works to which I am particularly indebted. I could not have written on *Ulysses* at all without the work of Joyceans like Robert M. Adams, Richard Ellmann, Don Gifford, and Hugh Kenner. On their explications of the novel I have drawn repeatedly, and it is a pleasure to acknowledge my gratitude to them here.

It is a pleasure also to remember the guidance of the late Darcy O'Brien and to thank David Thorburn for his Joycean teaching. I am indebted to John Clark Elder, William Oram, and Michael Gorra for criticism of preliminary versions of this book. My students too, at Yale and Smith, have taught me at least as much about *Ulysses* as I have managed to impart to them; I am particularly grateful for ideas and comments made by Stephanie Schoen.

Reproduction of excerpts from *Ulysses, A Portrait of the Artist as a Young Man,* and letters of James Joyce is by permission of the Estate of James Joyce, © Copyright, Estate of James Joyce. The Outline of *Ulysses,* used by permission of Alfred A. Knopf, a division of Random House, Inc., and Faber & Faber, Ltd., adapts a version first published in *James Joyce's Ulysses* by Stuart Gilbert, copyright 1930, 1952 by Stuart Gilbert, copyright renewed 1958 by Arthur Stuart Gilbert.

Contents

Preface

THIS BOOK is intended for first-time readers of *Ulysses*. In planning it, I have kept in mind the difficulties with the novel such readers actually face and the questions they are likely to have. Anything that might seriously interfere with a pleasurable reading of one of the most pleasure-giving books ever written I have tried to account for and explain. But I have not explained everything, not tracked every allusion relentlessly to its source, every symbol to its explication, every inconsistency to its significance (or non-significance). Even if I were capable of doing such a thing, I would not: a guidebook explicating every mystery of *Ulysses* would be grotesquely long and appallingly dull. First-time readers need to explicate some mysteries for themselves; they need to start learning how to be Joycean. If this book makes that sort of reading possible, it will have accomplished its purpose.

Following this Preface is an Introduction discussing such Joycean techniques as the Homeric parallel, interior monologue, and multiple narrative styles and specifying a few techniques—a few ways of paying attention and remaining patient—readers need to bring to their encounters with the novel. Readers also need a general sense of where *Ulysses* is going, and by way of road map I have supplied a version of the Outline of the novel which Joyce made available to his friend and early commentator Stuart Gilbert. Following that, the Guide to the Events of June 16, 1904, on pages 23–104 is a description of what happens in the plot of *Ulysses*. It is meant to help first-time readers understand what they must know as they make their way, along with the characters, from the morning to the evening (and beyond) of a long and sometimes exhausting fictional day. Chapter by chapter it glosses words, identifies references to Irish culture and history, translates foreign phrases, comments on character, and simply summarizes events. I have also provided brief summaries of events in the *Odyssey*, since it was on this ancient narrative that Joyce patterned the events of his fictional day in Dublin, June 16, 1904. A good many Joycean critics, beginning with Ezra Pound, have regarded the Homeric parallel as being useful chiefly to Joyce himself, a sort of temporary scaffold enabling him to erect the vast structure of the novel, but I take it more seriously than that and have tried to show how a knowledge of its details can aid readers, including first-time readers.

After six hundred and forty-four pages of Joycean happenings, the characters reach their ambiguous final destinies, and the novel comes to an end. Thereupon the question becomes not how to read *Ulysses*, but why. What does the book amount to when seen whole? All who have read through to the last page will have thought of answers to this question; in a brief Afterword I give some answers that occur to me.

Introduction

Preparations

HOW SHOULD you read *Ulysses*? It would be a good idea to begin, as most readers do, with Joyce's earlier works of fiction, the short story collection *Dubliners* (1914) and the semi-autobiographical novel *A Portrait of the Artist as a Young Man* (1916). The first introduces you to Joyce's setting, the second to the early life of Stephen Dedalus, one of the three major figures of *Ulysses*. As time permits you might also read at least the first half of Homer's *Odyssey*, in which the hero defeats monsters and evades dangers (and temptations) on his way home to Ithaca. There are particular pleasures to be had in discovering for yourself the devices, some of them extraordinarily ingenious, by which Joyce rewrote Homer for the twentieth century. All that done, proceed to the novel itself, which since 1986 has been available in a text corrected by Hans Walter Gabler and others and published by Random House. Almost from the moment of its appearance, a bibliographical controversy has raged about the corrected *Ulysses*. There are mistakes in it (misspellings of well-known Dublin names, for example), and it should not be taken as perfect, but the new edition of *Ulysses* improves on the older ones and, until a better appears, is the text to use.

When you are actually reading the novel, you should consult the relevant section of the Guide to the Events of June 16, 1904, before beginning each new chapter, and at a single sitting you should get through a substantial portion of the book—at least a whole chapter or a long stretch of one of the later, longer chapters—in order to see how Joyce has made these major divisions of his book stylistically and thematically consistent. You should of course go carefully through Joyce's prose itself. It needs care. But you should not proceed with unnatural slowness or worry unduly about details that remain obscure after attentive reading. Your task is to read a novel with alert curiosity, not solve a puzzle with dogged persistence. In any case, *Ulysses* rewards patience. Much that is initially unclear will be less so later, when Joyce sets his characters to remembering (and clarifying for themselves) what has already happened to them.

Gerty MacDowell as a character in a novel

"People like him because he is incomprehensible," Gertrude Stein said of the author of *Ulysses*, and with a fine show of illogic she added "and anybody can understand him."[1]   In Paris, where the novel was published under the imprint of the Shakespeare & Company Bookshop in 1922, its alleged incomprehensibility might have seemed admirable, even obligatory. Stein and others were at that moment publicizing literary Modernism and making new demands on the patience of readers. But incomprehensibility has not remained the chief reason for liking Joyce and his novel; it's the second part of Stein's statement, not the first, which now seems right. Thanks to the labors of hundreds of scholars, labors maintained over more than seven decades since 1922, a great many Joycean problems have been solved, a great many darknesses illuminated. Anybody can understand *Ulysses*.

The work of understanding begins with adjusting expectations, which means identifying the literary company *Ulysses* keeps. Where are its affinities? With *Madame Bovary* and *Anna Karenina* or other masterworks of nineteenth-century novelistic realism which Joyce deeply admired? With the *Odyssey* or the *Divine Comedy*? With *Gargantua and Pantagruel* and *Tristram Shandy*, eccentric comedies of verbal extravagance? With T. S. Eliot's *Waste Land* and Ezra Pound's *Cantos*? With *Thom's Dublin Post Office Directory* for 1904?

We can formulate an answer by turning from Gertrude Stein to Gertrude MacDowell, a sentimental Dublin maiden whom you will meet in the thirteenth chapter of *Ulysses*. There Joyce transcribes Gerty's copious

---

1. Richard Ellmann, *James Joyce*, new and revised ed. (Oxford and New York: Oxford University Press, 1982), p. 529. Ellmann's magisterial biography is a primary resource for anyone seriously interested in Joyce. Perhaps Stein's claim is valid if she means by it that you can say anything you like about a genuinely incomprehensible work.

thoughts—she is on a beach at dusk, in a pensive mood. The following passage is representative:

> And she could see far away the lights of the lighthouses so picturesque she would have loved to do with a box of paints because it was easier than to make a man and soon the lamplighter would be going his rounds past the presbyterian church grounds and along by shady Tritonville avenue where the couples walked and lighting the lamp near her window where Reggy Wylie used to turn his freewheel like she read in that book *The Lamplighter* by Miss Cummins, author of *Mabel Vaughan* and other tales. For Gerty had her dreams that no-one knew of. She loved to read poetry and when she got a keepsake from Bertha Supple of that lovely confession album with the coralpink cover to write her thoughts in she laid it in the drawer of her toilettable which, though it did not err on the side of luxury, was scrupulously neat and clean. It was there she kept her girlish treasure trove, the tortoiseshell combs, her child of Mary badge, the whiterose scent, the eyebrowleine, her alabaster pouncetbox and the ribbons to change when her things came home from the wash and there were some beautiful thoughts written in it in violet ink that she bought in Hely's of Dame Street for she felt that she too could write poetry if she could only express herself like that poem that appealed to her so deeply that she had copied out of the newspaper she found one evening round the potherbs. *Art thou real, my ideal?* it was called by Louis J Walsh, Magherafelt… (13.627).[1]

Here, with the freedom novelists have always enjoyed, Joyce moves in and out of Gerty's mind, creating her equally of things (the child of Mary badge), of thoughts (she has her dreams), and of a breathless, cliché-ridden style in which the thoughts take form. And he creates her of narrated actions, though in the quoted lines, as it happens, she does little but look to the distant picturesque lights. Putting this passage about Gerty together with others, we assemble a personality just as defined as those found in the pages of *Madame Bovary* and *Anna Karenina*. Gerty begins to sound to us like Gerty, like no one else in the book. In her things we read particular social circumstances, in her thoughts a mental condition. In short, we apprehend her as a "character." Moreover, we apprehend how the thoughts and actions of several characters become linked in sequences of cause-and-effect: "plots." Gerty is wistful because Reggy Wylie has ceased to notice her; she savors her love of poetry because others (girlfriends on the beach

---

1. In each parenthetical citation I have given *line numbers*, preceding these with the chapter number when the chapter is not obvious from the context. All quotations are taken from *Ulysses*, the corrected text, ed. Hans Walter Gabler, with Wolfhard Steppe and Claus Melchior (New York: Random House, 1986).

with her, for example) seem to misjudge her. Employing an ordinary novelist's skills—he has these in abundance, together with more remarkable gifts—Joyce makes the character, the other characters, the immediate moment, the remembered past, the guessed-at future, all belong to a single consistent world, and this world seems enough like those we inhabit ourselves to be intelligible and entertaining. Who has not written down, with or without the aid of violet ink, "beautiful thoughts"?

What is true of Gerty is true of the greater figures of the book. Leopold Bloom, his wife Molly, and Stephen Dedalus are characters inhabiting a thoroughly realized fictional world and acting according to motives we can, for the most part, learn to understand. (In the thirteenth chapter Bloom ogles Gerty on the beach, doing so because he is lonely, because he feels old, because he no longer enjoys a sexual relation with his wife.) In this most basic sense of providing characters and plots, *Ulysses* is a novel. Out of words it creates plausible versions of men and women: a harder task, as Gerty observes, than creating pure landscape.

This is a fact to be remembered amid all the complexities you will encounter, especially in the later chapters of the book, when Joyce's purposes multiply and for long stretches he seems to lose sight of characters and plots alike. Influenced by these later chapters, and by undeniable inconsistencies in Joyce's relating of events, some recent Joycean critics have argued against regarding *Ulysses* as a more or less reliable literary imitation of the "real" world, or a world that was real in 1904—in short, as a novel at all. This view seems to me limiting and one-sided ("one-eyed," Joyce might have said, with Homer's Cyclops in mind), in that it refuses to acknowledge what generations of readers have found in Joyce's pages, a general consistency in the characters and events presented, a consistency able to survive a quite remarkable number of Joycean cross-purposes and minor discrepancies.

This is not to say that you should take *Ulysses* as a straightforward transcription of reality (an equally limited and one-sided view) or even expect it to resemble conventional realistic novels. Compared with ordinary fiction, *Ulysses* is tricky, playful, artificial, and insistent that its artifice should be recognized. More obviously yet, it is unexplanatory and makes new demands on the reader. You must infer from a few passing references in *Nausicaa* that Gerty has a soft spot for Reggy Wylie. Joyce says nothing about it directly, preferring as always dramatic presentation to authoritative commentary. The fully evolved artist "remains within or behind or beyond or above his handiwork, invisible, refined out of existence," Joyce has the young Stephen Dedalus say in *A Portrait of the Artist as a Young Man.*[1] Joyce unquestionably shares the desire for authorial invisibility, though one can see him distancing himself from many of Stephen's other opinions, and though even with this one there are one or two exceptions to be made.

In practice, you will not find it difficult to infer characters' feelings in *Ulysses.* For instance, you will readily diagnose Gerty's melancholy as she watches Reggy and his "freewheel" out her window of an evening. What gives somewhat more trouble is the sheer density of the fictional world which the characters inhabit. In nearly every sentence *Ulysses* sets items or actions of ordinary life before us. No one of them is crucial by itself, but each invites consideration. Take "freewheel," for example. The mere name sounds appropriate enough, counterpointed as it obviously is against Gerty's having to stay in her house with Bertha Supple's keepsake for her only company, in a life bounded on one side by "Art thou real, my ideal?" and on the other by the potherbs. But what exactly is this freewheeling vehicle she recalls? What does the possession of a freewheel tell us about Reggy Wylie and his accessibility or inaccessibility to Gerty? Furthermore where in the Dublin of 1904 was Tritonville Avenue and which couples liked to walk along it, doing what? How does the child of Mary badge place Gerty in a certain category of Catholic piety?

Much about Dublin, its vehicles, its citizens, its turn-of-the-century gossip, its drinking and worshipping habits, its songs, its long political memory, and its mercantile life will seem reasonably familiar to you if, before approaching *Ulysses,* you read *A Portrait of the Artist* and *Dubliners.* Joycean reference books will answer some remaining questions, fully or partially.[2] In the Guide to the Events of June 16, 1904, I have glossed many of the most interesting features of Joyce's fictional world myself. Nevertheless you should not be dismayed if details, even many details, stay obstinately in a place and a time not your own, refusing to yield up their

1. *The Portable James Joyce,* ed. Harry Levin (New York: Penguin, 1966), p. 483.

2. By far the most useful work is Don Gifford with Robert J. Seidman, *Ulysses Annotated: Notes for James Joyce's Ulysses,* revised edition (Berkeley: University of California Press, 1988). You should turn first to Gifford and Seidman for topographical facts, lyrics of songs, translations of foreign languages, Irishisms, sources of quotations, and descriptions of period objects, e.g., "freewheel—in 1904, a relatively 'modern' bicycle, equipped with a clutch that would disengage the rear wheel except when the driver was pedaling forward" (p. 393).

significance, if any. Using *Thom's Directory* (a volume to which he was as devoted as to any nineteenth-century novel) and the memories of all his relatives,[1] Joyce saturated *Ulysses* with the life of Dublin in 1904. He saturated it as no novelist before him had done with a setting, saturated it beyond the capacity of any commentator to annotate completely and of anyone to comprehend in a single reading.

Joyce and Homer

Joyce said that he wrote the *Dubliners* stories in a style of "scrupulous meanness." This is an apt phrase for his flat, clinical observation of characters severely limited by circumstances, whose various states of timidity, ignorance, poverty, or drunkenness are laid out plentifully if somewhat cold-bloodedly before the reader.

"Scrupulous meanness" will not however do for any of the styles of *Ulysses*. In the novel Joyce attempts more ambitious linguistic maneuvers and takes a more generous view of his characters. Though their failings are still on display—Joyce puts the ungrammatical "used to turn his freewheel like she read in that book" into Gerty's mind—those failings do not seem the essential thing about them. They have unexpected qualities and relations, so that we cannot feel for them, as we do for many characters in the short stories, only pity mixed with contempt.

The characters of *Ulysses*, in other words, sometimes manage to escape the Dublin which circumscribes their lives. They do so most obviously when, remaining in the Irish city, they move into the Greek past. That is, they escape when Joyce makes them Homeric. Gerty MacDowell is the princess Nausicaa of the *Odyssey*, as the title of the chapter in which she figures announces.[2] Leopold Bloom is Odysseus or Ulysses (the Latin form

---

1. "I want that information about the Star of the Sea Church [a feature of *Nausicaa*], has it ivy on its seafront, are there trees in Leahy's terrace at the side or near, if so, what are these steps leading down to the beach? I also want all the information you can give, tittletattle, facts etc about Hollis Street maternity hospital. Two chapters of my book remain unfinished till I have these..." Joyce in an early 1920 letter to his aunt Josephine Murray, published in *Letters of James Joyce*, ed. Stuart Gilbert (New York: Viking, 1957), I, 136.

2. Or as it announces if you know the chapter titles. Joyce devised them all but then removed them from the first edition of *Ulysses*, perhaps to make the parallels less obvious. Nevertheless they were used by Joyce in correspondence, have routinely been employed by critics, and will be used here.

of the name), the hero of the epic. Molly Bloom is Penelope, his wife. Stephen Dedalus is Telemachus, his son. The events of *Ulysses* parallel the events of Homer's ancient narrative, with appropriate twentieth-century substitutions—for a fight with the one-eyed giant Polyphemus, a quarrel with a barroom bigot; for a voyage to the underworld, a funeral in a Dublin cemetery.

Though it lacks some of the usual epic conventions, such as interactions of gods and men, funeral games, digressive similes, a consistently elevated tone, and the like, *Ulysses* is nevertheless an epic, and not just in the Cecil B. DeMille sense (cast of hundreds, elaborate period details, seven years in the writing). Joyce's novel becomes an epic in the process of imitating one. Without ever ceasing to be comic, it gains complexity and seriousness by rehearsing themes—the overcoming of brutality and treachery, the recovery of place and possessions, the exploration of human destiny—which worthy epic predecessors have rehearsed. In an act of mingled piety and arrogance, Joyce revises Homer, exactly as Virgil revised Homer or Milton revised Virgil.

All of this is hinted at, of course, in the title *Ulysses*—one place where Joyce does comment on his work authoritatively. Once you take the hint, what you learn is, first, how to anticipate events, and thus how to bring order to them. If you know at the start of the *Cyclops* chapter that Bloom is Ulysses and the bigot is Polyphemus, and if you remember that in the *Odyssey* Ulysses escapes Polyphemus by brains rather than brawn, then you will be expecting braininess in Bloom, which he duly demonstrates by way of attempted changes of subject and a quick exit. Moreover at the very end of the chapter Bloom ventures a foolhardy taunt, nearly leading to catastrophe (the bigot hurls a biscuitbox at him), exactly as happens with Ulysses (Polyphemus hurls a boulder). By means of hundreds of such Homeric correspondences Joyce encourages you to guess at what is coming and comprehend what has happened. You learn how to follow the story because you have heard something like it before.

This is the technique which T. S. Eliot seems to have had in mind when, in a famous early review of *Ulysses*, he identified Joyce's "mythical method":

> In using the myth, in manipulating a continuous parallel between contemporaneity and antiquity, Mr. Joyce is pursuing a method which others must pursue after him…It is simply a way of controlling, of ordering, of giving a shape and a significance to the immense panorama of futility and anarchy which is

contemporary history...It is a method for which the horoscope is auspicious. Psychology (such as it is, and whether our reaction to it be comic or serious), ethnology, and *The Golden Bough* have concurred to make possible what was impossible even a few years ago. Instead of the narrative method, we may now use the mythical method.[1]

Eliot's contemptuous words "the immense panorama of futility and anarchy which is contemporary history" raise the possibility of Homer's being used in a different, evaluative way. In *Ulysses*, does the *Odyssey* provide a genuinely heroic background—a standard of judgment—against which Joyce shows up twentieth-century life in all its shabbiness and spurious heroism? In this view, a fairly widely held one, Polyphemus' boulder makes the bigot's biscuitbox look ludicrous, and all the other Homeric correspondences work similarly. In effect, the claim goes, we put ironic quotation marks around all our identifications: Bloom "is" Ulysses, Gerty "is" Nausicaa, but over and over again they fail to live up to their assigned roles. So interpreted, Joyce's characters would join ranks with Eliot's J. Alfred Prufrock ("I am not Prince Hamlet") and Pound's Hugh Selwyn Mauberley, those familiar denizens of what Pound called a "botched civilization."

No one would deny that Joyce's world is more anarchic than Homer's. No goddess Athena appears at the end of *Ulysses* (as she does in the *Odyssey*) to stop bloodshed with an authoritative moral judgment. Nor would anyone deny that Joyce's characters often look modern, ordinary, silly, shabby. While gazing at Gerty, Bloom masturbates—not something we catch Ulysses or Aeneas doing. But I would deny that the characters are *primarily* exhibits in an indictment of the botched twentieth century. They are more complicated than that. Simultaneously comic and heroic, shabby and impressive, they make humanity rather than divinity manifest, and in the process they furnish lessons in historical continuity. As you have seen, Gerty MacDowell reads cheap novels and believes in the powers of eyebrowleine; she is what contemporary lower-middle-class Irish life has made her. But at the same time she is what centuries of European culture have made her, as much a product of that culture as her ancient namesake Nausicaa, whose attributes—innocence, pluck, and a longing for romance,

---

1. "*Ulysses*, Order, and Myth," first published in *The Dial* (1923) and reprinted widely, e.g., in *The Modern Tradition*, ed. Richard Ellmann and Charles Feidelson (New York: Oxford University Press, 1965), p. 681. *The Golden Bough*: Sir James Frazer's compendious study (1890) of fertility myths and rituals.

especially romance involving a mysterious stranger older than herself—she shares. In Gerty these qualities are made continuous from ancient Greece to modern Ireland, and thus she embodies one of Joyce's most tenacious beliefs, that the present repeats the past. Similarly, the present repeats the past in Bloom's Ulysses-like versatility or Stephen's Telemachus-like resentment. "As it was in the beginning, is now…and ever shall be," Joyce allows Stephen to think in an early chapter (*Nestor*, 200), using a familiar formula to drive his point about continuity home. Later, more elaborately, Stephen contemplates "the now, the here, through which all future plunges to the past" (*Scylla and Charybdis*, 89). In *Ulysses* the future is always plunging to the past, or Joyce is giving it a gentle push in that direction, so that we will recognize how familiar it looks.

To emphasize historical continuities and employ "the mythical method," Joyce might have imitated any old narrative. Indeed, he briefly imitated several of them, when for example he shaped Stephen's situation to resemble Prince Hamlet's or Bloom's to resemble Rip Van Winkle's. Joyce's bookshelf had a good many volumes on it. Nevertheless, for his main parallel he turned to Homer and the *Odyssey*, chiefly because he greatly admired the hero of that particular epic. Ulysses, as he remarked on more than one occasion, is a man of varied skills, not just a warrior. He is prudent, resourceful, and eloquent. Furthermore, as a family man, he is a fitting counterpart for a modern-day hero Joyce wished (for a variety of reasons) to make Jewish. "They are better husbands than we are," Joyce said of Jews, "better fathers and better sons."[1]

The problem Joyce faced was finding a way to endorse these personal and familial virtues. He could scarcely admire them openly; aside from his disinclination to comment authoritatively, he wrote *Ulysses* at a time profoundly skeptical of heroism and weary of all the virtues openly admired by past writers. He therefore hid Ulyssean virtues away in the somewhat unlikely person of Leopold Bloom, where you can detect them underneath the more obvious foibles of the man, the masturbation and the superstition, the ignorance and the complacency, but only if you read perceptively, taking Homer as a guide. This is a strategy which Umberto Eco, an Italian semiotician and authority on Joyce, claims postmodern writers—the sophisticated heirs of Joyce—have invented. Eco imagines a man "who loves a very cultivated woman and knows he cannot say to her, 'I love you

---

1. Ellmann, *James Joyce*, p. 373, quoting a remark made to Joyce's friend Frank Budgen.

madly,' because he knows that she knows (and that she knows that he knows) that these words have already been written by Barbara Cartland." The solution, according to Eco, is to say "As Barbara Cartland would put it, I love you madly." The man will have avoided false innocence, "said clearly that it is no longer possible to speak innocently," but nevertheless conveyed his message: he loves the woman, and loves her in an age of lost innocence.[1] In fact, the age of lost innocence extends farther back than our postmodernist times, at least as far back as 1914–1922, the years of the writing of *Ulysses*. Like Eco's sophisticates, Joyce uses the innocent past to convey messages to the knowing present. In his twentieth-century epic he "says," in effect, "As Homer would put it, intelligence rises superior to brute strength, monsters may be defeated, after long travails heroes come home again."

Interior monologue

Joyce probably shared T. S. Eliot's skepticism about the new sciences of mind being organized in the first decades of the century. He certainly was skeptical about Freud and psychoanalysis. Yet like Freud he recorded his own dreams, and his writings make strenuous efforts to investigate the most private workings of the mind. In *Ulysses* the principal means of investigation is the narrative technique called interior monologue or stream of consciousness. This Joyce did not invent (he adapted it from a number of writers, especially the French novelist Édouard Dujardin), but in *Ulysses* he developed its possibilities with unparalleled thoroughness.

Interior monologue is not literally thinking, any more than the phrase "girlish treasure trove" is literally a collection of material objects owned by Gerty MacDowell. It is a representation, a stylization, of thinking, which uses short, often fragmentary phrases to give an impression of the characters' on-going mental lives. Omitting transitions and explanations (do you explain what you already know to yourself?), interior monologue dramatizes present moments of partial understanding and rapidly changing interests; the present tense, in fact, is one of its chief identifying characteristics. When in *Lestrygonians* Joyce writes "A blind stripling stood

---

1. *Postscript to The Name of the Rose*, tr. William Weaver (San Diego: Harcourt Brace Jovanovich, 1984), p. 67. Barbara Cartland, the late romance novelist, might be among Gerty MacDowell's favorites if Gerty were reading today.

tapping the curbstone with his slender cane," he is employing a perfectly conventional past-tense narrative, but when he adds "No tram in sight. Wants to cross" (8.1075), shifting into Bloom's observant mind via the truncated, present-tense last phrase, he is employing interior monologue.

The technique represents no radical departure from previous methods of entering and displaying fictional characters' minds, such as the *style indirect libre* of Flaubert and other nineteenth-century novelists, which freely paraphrases and mimics thinking. The lines from *Nausicaa* quoted at the start of this introduction paraphrase Gerty's thinking and give you an acquaintance with her secrets; with a few minor changes we could translate any particular passage—

> And she could see far away the lights of the lighthouses so picturesque she would have loved to do with a box of paints because it was easier than to make a man…

—into interior monologue:

> Can see the lights of the lighthouses, so picturesque! Love to do them with a box of paints. Easier than to make a man…

Still, the "she" and the past-tense verbs of Joyce's actual text have a specific effect, which is to put Gerty at a little distance from us, in a place where her creator has understood her thoroughly and now relates that understanding to us. She seems fixed, summed up. By contrast, when you read "Wants to cross" or "Wonder if he has a name" or any of the other interior-monologue phrases with which Bloom regards the blind man, you seem to be witnessing thought without Joyce's intervention. You seem to be brought intimately close to the character. Bloom, such is the effect of interior monologue, appears more capable of change than Gerty and more elusive of categorization.

The assignment of one narrative treatment to him and another to her is of course not accidental. It suits Joyce's purposes to keep Gerty and other minor characters at a little distance while bringing Bloom, Molly, and Stephen as close to us as possible; he reports their thought in enormous abundance.[1] All three major characters have inventive minds; all are curious

---

1. A few minor characters of *Ulysses* are given passages of interior monologue but only brief ones. Significantly, Joyce withholds even this privilege from Stephen's enemy Buck Mulligan and Bloom's enemy Blazes Boylan, as if to demonstrate their mental inferiority.

(though curious about different things); all are unconventional. Joyce's decision not to sum any one of them up, but rather to follow the shifting directions of their thoughts, patiently and scrupulously, as they move about Dublin or through personal memory, is the single most important factor in distinguishing *Ulysses* from previous works of fiction. The sheer quantity of interior monologue in the novel is audacious, ground-breaking, "Joycean."

The phrases about the blind man typify Bloom's thinking, which often derives from something sensed in the exterior world, often sympathizes, and often moves quickly on to something else. Stephen's interior monologues characteristically dwell in the world of books and ideas from which he is trying half-heartedly to escape. They are intellectual, sometimes esoterically intellectual, and therefore harder to follow than Bloom's monologues. Three quarters of the way down page one of the novel, you will encounter from Stephen the first bit of interior monologue in *Ulysses*, the one-word sentence "Chrysostomos." Apparently it refers to Buck Mulligan, one of the characters in the opening scene. The Greek word means "golden-mouthed," as a biographical dictionary would tell you, and was applied to the ancient rhetorician Dion Chrysostomos and the early Church Father St John Chrysostomos. Now, how should you apply this information? The hint at St John may be a sly Joycean touch, a private joke, because the real-life doctor on whom Mulligan was based was named Oliver St John Gogarty. But there are more accessible meanings at hand. Buck Mulligan has gold fillings in his teeth and speaks glibly; literally and figuratively, he is golden-mouthed. Moreover, the term "Chrysostomos" comes quite plausibly from Stephen Dedalus. He, not Joyce, thinks it. As a Jesuit-educated, lapsed-but-not-forgetting intellectual Catholic, Stephen knows a good deal about Church Fathers. As a poor man with bad teeth, he notices a well-to-do man with expensive dental work. These meanings of "Chrysostomos" may be obscure the first time you read *Ulysses* and may occasion some effort on your part, but they are not willfully obscure. Joyce does not deliberately hide them from you. He gives them to you in the unexplained form in which Stephen conceives them and, ultimately, therefore, helps you understand Stephen.

Molly's thinking, which furnishes the entire substance of the last chapter, dwells on private experience (she is in bed, remembering) and though characteristically sustained in phrasing (Molly, a singer, would say *legato*), it shifts from topic to topic with apparent abruptness:

> I made him blush a little when I got over him that way when I unbuttoned him and took his out and drew back the skin it had a kind of eye in it theyre all Buttons men down the middle on the wrong side of them Molly darling he called me what was his name Jack Joe Harry Mulvey was it yes (18.814).

Molly recalls an intimate moment with an early lover, then notes that men's garments have buttons on the wrong side (i.e., not the same side as women's garments), then goes back to "Jack Joe Harry." You could ascribe this odd digression merely to Molly's clothes sense (she once did a little business in second-hand apparel), but there is a subtler connection between thoughts to be discovered. As you will see, Molly savors again and again the differences between men and women, the biological differences from which she derives sexual pleasure, the social differences which often provoke her scorn. Men love her, men blush, men have buttons on the wrong side: the three observations are really the same observation about the other sex, which fascinates and amuses Molly in equal measure.

The first reward of reading interior monologue comes from just this sort of reading between the lines, from finding connections between apparently unrelated thoughts. The second comes from completing thoughts which characters cannot admit fully—as when Bloom, acknowledging his daughter's sexual precocity, allows only the vague words "Will happen, yes" to emerge into consciousness (4.447). The connections and completions take you deep into the essential lives of Bloom, Molly, and Stephen, into the mental arena where their real battles, the ones between evasion and honesty, have to be fought. But you should not for this reason assume that interior monologue is always to be interpreted in a spirit of solemn psychological analysis. Joyce was a connoisseur of accidental, amusing mental associations and filled his novel with them. Nothing could be more typical, for example, than an association Bloom makes as he tries to remember a word on the tip of his tongue. In *Calypso*, Molly asks her husband about the mysterious foreign term "metempsychosis." It means the "transmigration of souls," he says, but cannot find the synonym he wants until a few lines later:

> Must get that Capel street library book renewed or they'll write to Kearney, my guarantor. Reincarnation: that's the word (4.360).

Give the guarantor's name its Irish pronunciation ("Carney"), and you will see exactly how Bloom's thinking proceeds. Here, and in a gratifyingly large number of other instances, following a train of thought means joining in a linguistic game, listening to the plays on sounds and notions by which the characters (Bloom usually, but not exclusively) make their comic way from one idea to another. "Listening," incidentally, is often best done literally: the obscurity of many Joycean passages melts away when you read them aloud.

World versus word

Before meeting Gerty, Bloom reads a letter from another young woman, Martha Clifford, with whom he is carrying on a dalliance-by-mail. Apparently shocked (though also titillated) by something Bloom has written, Martha explains that she has called him "naughty boy" because she does not like "that other word" (5.245). That, at least, is what she means to type, but on paper the phrase comes out "that other world." Bloom remembers the error later; it helps him make a key decision.

Martha's "world" and "word" give us convenient terms for the two fundamental elements of fiction, and the fact that she confuses them hints at how intricately they are involved with each other. "World" stands for everything a novel represents—a setting, its inhabitants, their actions, their thoughts—while "word" stands for the prose by which the representation is accomplished. When you read run-of-the-mill fiction, you devote much more attention to the world represented than to the author's words in themselves, which work (or do not work) with simple efficiency to get you to the dramatic denouement or the happy ending. In the prose of more ambitious novelists, words assert themselves and provide an esthetic pleasure of their own, often in ways that you can confidently describe as an individual authorial style—Faulkner's style, D. H. Lawrence's style, Hemingway's style. With Joyce, the most ambitious of them all, you encounter nothing so easily categorizable but rather multiple styles, assemblages of words carefully matched with individual human beings. "Joycean" language turns out to be Bloomian language, Dedalian language, Mollyesque language, or the language of any of the minor personages who stand forth for a moment to enrich your sense of Dublin types. These styles of *Ulysses* insist on being noticed; appreciating them for what they are is a large part of your task as reader.

The gushing language at the start of *Nausicaa*, for example, is unquestionably the first noticeable thing in the chapter. No mere efficient means of giving you Gerty MacDowell, it is an essential part of this young woman who fashions herself after magazine prose. One might say that to create Gerty, Joyce *merges* word with world, doing deliberately what Martha Clifford does accidentally, and in countless other passages of *Ulysses* he performs the same trick. He makes language and personality indistinguishable, describing characters' actions in the language they themselves would use if they were narrators.[1]

Even more remarkably, Joyce makes language and outward circumstance indistinguishable, or at least demonstrates how the latter shapes the former. In *Wandering Rocks* you will overhear some of the thoughts of Father John Conmee, an influential Jesuit superior. Father Conmee recalls reading his divine office when he was rector of Clongowes Wood School, and his memory of that episode in his life—"He was their rector: his reign was mild" (188)—emerges in the sonorous, parallel style of the very texts he read, the psalms in his breviary. Here, the language of a character's thought adapts itself to a circumstance of the world in which that character is momentarily situated. So with many of the people of *Ulysses*. When Stephen invokes Aristotle by the sobriquet *maestro di color che sanno*, "master of them that know" (3.6), he is quoting a familiar phrase from Dante, but whether he knows it consciously or not he is also punning between Italian and English. That is, he is responding to the idea of color, which at present—"Snotgreen, bluesilver, rust: coloured signs"—occupies his teeming mind.

You will discover many places in *Ulysses* where Joyce's own narrative language adapts itself to current circumstances, to whatever is important or striking in the immediate context. In all the voices he uses to describe action Joyce shows himself to be flexibly adaptable, a chameleon of a narrator. On a small scale, for instance, he narrates the exit of a cemetery caretaker in a style unmistakably mimicking the high solemnity of an epic: "Quietly, sure of his ground, he traversed the dismal fields" (6.876). It is as though Joyce has been overwhelmed by the Homeric parallel he himself has set up in *Hades*, between Ulysses' visit to the shades and Bloom's attendance at Paddy Dignam's funeral, and has been compelled, for the duration of a single sentence, to write epically. (It should be noted that *Hades* is a chapter bringing the Homeric parallel particularly to the fore.)

---

1. This is the Joycean technique which Hugh Kenner has wittily explained and dubbed "the Uncle Charles principle," after an early use of it in *A Portrait of the Artist*. See *Joyce's Voices* (Berkeley and Los Angeles: University of California Press, 1978), pp. 15–38.

On a larger scale in later chapters, Joyce narrates barroom concertizing in language imitating musical devices (*Sirens*) and late-night wandering in language itself wandering and repetitive (*Eumaeus*). In these imitative styles matter comes together with manner in a particularly Joycean harmony. "The phrase and the day and the scene harmonised in a chord," he puts it in a sentence from *A Portrait of the Artist*.[1]

By the time you reach the later chapters of the novel, you will be accustomed to imitative styles and adept at relating them to action. But you will also be accustomed to language in the form of pure virtuoso performance. As *Ulysses* proceeds, its styles tend to break free from Dublin happenings and go their own supremely inventive way. One chapter (*Aeolus*) furnishes a series of newspaper headlines ending in flamboyant magniloquence, one (*Ithaca*) a series of mock-formal questions and comically prolonged answers. Yet another (*Oxen of the Sun*) concludes with the most stupendous farrago of modern slang, cant, and dialect ever penned. The later chapters grow long with all the language they contain. Word does battle with world and apparently comes out victorious; Joyce the author appears plainly visible within his handiwork despite what Stephen says in the passage from *A Portrait*. He never announces himself as "Joyce," of course, but in all his linguistic variations he reveals the same shaping and self-advertising intelligence. Having refined himself out of existence to create characters and dramatic scenes, he refines himself back into existence via style.

The Joyce of the later pages of *Ulysses*—the heir of Rabelais and Sterne, not of Flaubert and Tolstoy—seems bent on exhausting the possibilities of words and their arrangement, or even letters and their arrangement, as in a list of anagrams provided for "Leopold Bloom":

Ellpodbomool
Molldopeloob
Bollopedoom
Old Ollebo, M.P. (17.404)

I have said that first-time readers need to learn to be Joycean. Part of what that means should now be clear. To be Joycean is to be entranced with language, *all* language, foreign and domestic, learned and popular, archaic

---

1. *The Portable James Joyce*, p. 428.

and contemporary, poetic and prosaic; language from anagrams like those above, to babble,

> Love loves to love love. Nurse loves the new chemist. Constable 14A loves Mary Kelly. Gerty MacDowell loves the boy that has the bicycle. M. B. loves a fair gentleman. Li Chi Han lovey up kissy Cha Pu Chow (12.1493),

to an elaborate rhetoric of paralleled but inverted phrases,

> Grossbooted draymen rolled barrels dullthudding out of Prince's stores and bumped them up on the brewery float. On the brewery float bumped dullthudding barrels rolled by grossbooted draymen out of Prince's stores (7.21),

to comic inventions of the music hall,

> *Corny Kelleher again reassuralooms with his hand. Bloom with his hand assuralooms Corny Kelleher that he is reassuraloomtay* (15.4917),

to vocabulary-building lists of synonyms,

> She trudges, schlepps, trains, drags, trascines her load (3.392),

to clever neologisms,

> endlessnessnessness .... (11.750),

to lines of a surpassing eloquence,

> The heaventree of stars hung with humid nightblue fruit (17.1039),

and to the dirty street rhymes of the Prison Gate Girls:

> If you see Kay,
> Tell him he may
> See you in tea
> Tell him from me (15.1893).[1]

Those reading *Ulysses* exclusively as a Flaubertian or Tolstoyan fiction may be distracted by so much linguistic playfulness on parade, perhaps even

---

1. Construe the first and third lines of this quatrain as letters, not words.

dismayed by it, as Ellpodbomool and Molldopeloob replace the sense of novelistic closure or consistent presentation of character they seek. Conversely, those reading *Ulysses* primarily as a word game will be pleased by the turn later chapters take, though they may miss much of what the novel has earlier offered, insisted on, by way of plot, character, and theme. For that matter they may miss the import of certain late passages. Sharing *Ithaca* with the anagrams on "Leopold Bloom" is a painstaking catalogue of dozens of objects in Bloom's locked drawer. Individual items here are jokes ("a pink ribbon which had festooned an Easter egg in the year 1899," 1803), or even word games ("the transliterated name and address of the addresser of the 3 letters in reversed alphabetic boustrophedonic punctated quadrilinear cryptogram," 1798). But the whole collection is a revelation of Bloom, a comprehensive and moving revelation, which sums up his existence in a random assortment of mementoes. It needs to be read as carefully, as "novelistically," as any descriptive passage in Balzac. In the drawer, pathetically, is the Ithaca our hero seeks, the possessions he is allowed to recover on coming home: two fading photographs, a press cutting of a recipe for the renovation of tan boots, a remedy for rectal complaints, an old sandglass.

For prospective readers of *Ulysses*, the moral is clear enough. A first-time reading should avoid exclusive expectations. You must go through Joyce's novel not with the one-eyed dogmatism of the bigot in *Cyclops* but with the two-eyed vision Bloom displays in the same chapter; you must attend equally to word and world. Doing so will not guarantee full comprehension—there is no guarantee of that, even on repeated re-readings—but it will make sustained pleasure likely. The notoriously complicated and difficult novel you are about to read is sometimes begun with foreboding. Given the right effort in reading, the right consideration of Gerty's phrasing and Reggy's freewheel, Homer's underworld and Dublin's cemetery, it will be read to the end with increasing admiration and then put down with reluctance.

Outline of *Ulysses*

THE OUTLINE that follows is adapted from a "Ground Plan" which Joyce furnished to his French translator and which was first published in Stuart Gilbert's pioneering (1931) study of *Ulysses*.[1] Anyone writing a novel as encyclopedically detailed as *Ulysses* might wish to schematize it, but Joyce was especially drawn to schemas and plans. From his Jesuit teachers, he said, he had learned to arrange things in such a way that they became easy to survey and to judge,[2] and while writing his novel he unquestionably had an elaborate arrangement of fictional elements in mind. Each chapter, for example, encompasses one particular intellectual endeavor or "art," which may be openly discussed, as with the medical topics of conversation in *Oxen of the Sun*, or which may simply be thought of or seen in operation. In *Lotus Eaters*, for example, Bloom contemplates medicinal plants and orders a skin lotion for Molly; hence its arts are botany and chemistry. The chapters are also devoted, literally or figuratively, to the various organs of the human body—a pork kidney Bloom eats for his breakfast in *Calypso*, the lungs supplying the wherewithal for windy speechifying in *Aeolus*. Just as Joyce was pleased to render the whole of a city and the whole of a single day, he was pleased to reproduce in his novel the full range of human artistic achievement and the complete human body, right down to esophagus and genitals.

Like *Ulysses* itself, the outline has its subtleties and obscurities. Why are no "organs" specified for the first three chapters of the novel? Because, Joyce hints, Stephen's body is much less important than his mind; real corporeality enters the novel only with Bloom. What does "economics"

---

1. See *James Joyce's Ulysses*, second ed. (New York: Knopf, 1952), p. 41. Gilbert's outline includes (for most chapters) the additional categories of "Color," "Symbol," and "Technic."

2. Ellmann, *James Joyce*, p. 27.

have to do with *Calypso?* As you will see, the chapter mentions prices and money but not more significantly than other chapters; Joyce is rather thinking of the root meaning of "economics" as the science of household management—a meaning particularly appropriate to *Calypso.*

*   *   *

Chapter	Place and time	Organ	Art

I: The Telemachiad (Stephen's Morning)

Chapter	Place and time	Organ	Art
[1] *Telemachus* 3–19	Martello tower, south of Dublin, 8 am		Theology
[2] *Nestor* 20–30	School in Dalkey, a Dublin suburb, 10 am		History
[3] *Proteus* 31–42	Sandymount strand on Dublin bay, 11 am		Philology

II: The Wanderings

Chapter	Place and time	Organ	Art
[4] *Calypso* 45–57	7 Eccles Street, Dublin, 8 am	Kidney	Economics
[5] *Lotus Eaters* 58–71	To the Baths, 10 am	Genitals	Botany, Chemistry
[6] *Hades* 72–95	To Prospect Cemetery, 11 am	Heart	Religion
[7] *Aeolus* 96–123	Newspaper office to Nelson's pillar, noon	Lungs	Rhetoric

Continued on next page...

[8] *Lestry-gonians* 124–150	To the pub, 1 pm	Esophagus	Architecture
[9] *Scylla and Charybdis* 151–179	National Library, 2 pm	Brain	Literature
[10] *Wandering Rocks* 180–209	Mostly the old city, 3 pm	Blood	Mechanics
[11] *Sirens* 210–239	Ormond Hotel, 4 pm	Ear	Music
[12] *Cyclops* 240–283	Kiernan's pub, 5 pm	Muscle	Politics
[13] *Nausicaa* 284–313	Sandymount strand, 8 pm	Eye, nose	Painting
[14] *Oxen of the Sun* 314–349	Holles Street Hospital, 10 pm	Womb	Medicine
[15] *Circe* 350–497	Nighttown: brothel, midnight	Locomotor apparatus	Magic

III: Nostos (the Return)

[16] *Eumaeus* 501–543	The cab shelter, 1 am	Nerves	Navigation
[17] *Ithaca* 544–607	7 Eccles Street, 2 am	Skeleton	Science
[18] *Penelope* 608–644	7 Eccles Street, after 2 am		Flesh

Guide to the Events of June 16, 1904

[1] *Telemachus* (pages 3–19)

Epics call for a certain grandeur, a certain formality of movement and gesture on the characters' and the author's part. It is therefore appropriate that the first word of Joyce's epic should be "stately." In the older editions of *Ulysses*, the word began with a giant, page-filling capital S, like one of the illuminated capitals in that other Irish masterpiece of intricate learning, the Book of Kells. But even without a giant initial, as we see it in the corrected *Ulysses*, the word sets a tone. Stately Buck Mulligan ushers us with formal pomp into a work which will attempt no less than the epic fictionalization of a single day and the bringing of Homer up to date.

Specifically, with the words *"Introibo ad altare Dei"* (5), Mulligan sounds the Introit for the Mass, which he proceeds to celebrate, mockingly. In the Mass, the priest holds up a wafer and by the magic of his voice turns it into Christ's body. In the six hundred and forty-four pages of his novel Joyce holds ordinary life up to our view and by the magic of his voice reveals the miraculous in it. The word "ordinary" needs stressing as much as "miraculous." After all, the second word of the book is "plump." *Ulysses* is modern, down-to-earth, observant. As much novel as epic, it plenteously fulfills the purpose which Joyce once said he would put on his artistic banner: "Describe what they do." (Much later, *Ulysses* explains Mulligan's plumpness by describing how he plasters butter on a scone and bites into it hungrily.)[1] However grand his formal and linguistic ambitions, Joyce never loses sight of the plump, hungry, tired, unwashed, inebriated, or otherwise human materials out of which he shapes his novel.

---

1. As it happens, Joyce made the remark to Oliver St John Gogarty, the real-life counterpart of Mulligan. See Richard Ellmann, *Ulysses on the Liffey*, p. 16. For Mulligan eating, see *Wandering Rocks*, 10.1087.

The first paragraphs of *Ulysses* seem modest enough in technique. Set before us is an understandable scene with apparently ordinary fictional characters, and with plausible dialogue (dialogue marked as direct speech by dashes, following the Continental convention which Joyce preferred). Only gradually are we introduced to the characters' thinking, in such scraps of interior monologue as "Chrysostomos" on page one (26) and "Parried again" on page six (152). From this point on we will witness more and more of Stephen's mental activity, until the third chapter, *Proteus*, will keep almost exclusively to interior monologue.

*   *   *

It is eight o'clock on the morning of June 16, 1904. Stephen Dedalus, returned home from eclectic studies in Paris, has taken up residence with Malachi (Buck) Mulligan, a medical student and wit, in the Martello tower overlooking Dublin bay at Sandycove, a few miles south of the city. In the clear morning light Mulligan and Stephen discuss the night just past. Haines, an Englishman devoted to things picturesquely Irish, is visiting the tower and has had a nightmare about a black panther. The two Irishmen look out over the sea, which Mulligan addresses in phrases taken from Algernon Charles Swinburne ("Algy") and Homer (*Epi oinopa ponton*, "over the wine-dark sea," 78). Mulligan is a quoter and parodist rather than a creator, a jester cavorting on the edges of the true comedy. He shaves, having borne with him to the top of the tower a mirror and a razor—the emblems of narcissism and cruelty, as we will later be able to read them. For now, they are plainly enough shaving utensils: at the start of his novel, Joyce's symbolism lies in hiding. Mulligan's symbolism, by contrast, goes on showy display. The lather in the shaving bowl he blasphemously transforms into the Host of a Mass. Christ becomes "Christine," Mulligan's two shrill whistles the Sanctus bell rung at the Elevation of the Host. "The mockery of it!" he says (34), laughing at his ability to laugh off everything.

From Stephen, Mulligan begs a handkerchief, the first of many borrowings in the novel. Mulligan will take money from Stephen, twopence in this chapter and more later, and the key of the Martello tower, for which Stephen has paid the rent. Stephen, meanwhile, is wearing Mulligan's secondhand trousers but will not accept the offer of a second, grey pair. He is in mourning for his mother and must, like Prince Hamlet, wear customary suits of solemn black. Mulligan, like King Claudius in

Shakespeare's play, scolds the young man for excessive mourning. He also scolds Stephen for refusing to kneel and pray at his mother's deathbed. There is talk of the shaving mirror—the symbol of realistic art, showing Ireland what it is. Perhaps the "oxy" chap downstairs (Haines is Oxonian, Saxon) will appreciate Stephen's well-turned phrase about the lookingglass. Mulligan admits his willingness to toady to the Englishman even while he expatiates on his schemes for Hellenising Ireland. "Why don't you play them as I do?" he asks Stephen a few pages later (506).

Stephen thinks briefly of a "ragging," undergraduate pranks at Oxford, then, freeing his arm, passes on to his elaborately cold snubbing of Mulligan, who has offended him with a crass remark about his mother being beastly dead. Stephen carefully manipulates this little scene: he provokes excuses from the voluble Mulligan, reserving for himself the last, crushing retort ("Of the offence to me," 220). Mulligan's real fault, perhaps, has been viewing death casually, which Stephen can never do. Now Stephen hears some verses from the W. B. Yeats lyric he sang to his dying mother, "Who Goes with Fergus?" "*And no more turn aside and brood*," Mulligan's booming voice counsels, but Stephen can never stop the moody brooding. A cloud covers the sun, turning Dublin bay into a bowl of bitter waters. Stephen thinks of his mother's pathetic treasures, then of her apparition haunting him in a dream, threatening him with piety and all-consuming maternal love. (Again, *Hamlet* comes to mind, with its ghostly parent forcing unwelcome obligations on an unhappy and dispossessed son.) The part of Stephen's mind that still belongs to his church and family recalls a sentence from the Latin prayer for the dying (*Liliata rutilantium te confessorum*, 276).[1] Immediately after, the part that is reaching out for mental independence— that refused the prayer when it would have eased his mother's death— accosts her ghost with "Ghoul! Chewer of corpses!" Stephen is both what he hopes to become in the future and what the past has made him: "I am another now and yet the same" (311).

Breakfast follows, downstairs: a simple enough event which yet confirms Stephen's distinctiveness in this household of young men. Mulligan tells a dialect joke, then, following a hint from Stephen, growls out a few lines of a bawdy song. The old milkwoman appears, bearing milk for their tea but speaking no Gaelic, as Haines discovers. "Poor old woman,"

---

1. "May the glittering throng of confessors, bright as lilies, gather about you. May the glorious choir of Virgins receive you." See Weldon Thornton, *Allusions in Ulysses* (Chapel Hill: Univ. of North Carolina Press, 1968), pp. 17–18.

like "silk of the kine," is a traditional epithet for Ireland: the milkwoman is
Ireland herself, bereft of her ancient language and culture. Note that this
identification is made in Stephen's mind: *he* sees the milkwoman as "an
immortal serving her conqueror" (404), just as later he sees her as a woman
with unclean loins, the serpent's prey, the temptress of Adam. Stephen is an
obsessive symbolist. He clothes what he sees in the high-colored trappings
of his national and religious patrimonies. Simultaneously he is jealous, in an
almost adolescent way: the old woman pays attention to Mulligan but
slights him, he observes.

The milk is paid for, partly, there is some casual talk about Stephen's
dislike of water, and the important phrase "Agenbite of inwit" floats into
Stephen's consciousness from a fourteenth-century treatise. Even disguised
in Middle English, the words mean something simple, "remorse of
conscience." Stephen guiltily remembers all that he did not do for his
mother and has not yet done for the poor old woman, and perhaps all he
has not yet done as a poet. He refuses to follow up Haines's suggestion
about making a collection of his sayings and so earns a brief rebuke from
Mulligan.

After the young men finish dressing, we follow them outside for a
scene which will develop the theme of refusals. Mulligan provides a
distorted version of Stephen's theory of that Shakespearean play which has
already figured largely, if secretly, in the chapter: *Hamlet*. Haines contributes
a bemused theological interpretation ("The Son striving to be atoned with
the Father," 578). Much more about fathers, sons, atonement, and *Hamlet*
will follow in the novel. Meanwhile Mulligan scampers away singing the
"Ballad of Joking Jesus." The conventional Haines, though not a believer,
laughs guardedly. Nor is Stephen a believer, but he resents having to make a
declaration of disbelief to Haines. He prefers to dwell with his own
thoughts: the key he will have to give up to Mulligan, the salt bread of exile
which he, like his brother poet Dante, will have to eat. Pairing himself with
Dante flatters Stephen's artistic ego. It also palliates his acknowledged
servitude to three masters: the Church, the British State, Ireland. It is
history which seems to blame for the Irish mess, Haines comments, but
Stephen, whose mind is full of the panoply of Catholicism—Latin titles
clanging like bells, Palestrina's music, heretics fleeing in disarray—scarcely
listens. Stephen recalls heretical doctrines in some detail, being a kind of
heretic himself.

At the swimming hole we hear of a drowned man, then, from a crony of Mulligan's in the water, of a "sweet young thing" (684) down in Westmeath—Milly, Bloom's daughter, as we will shortly learn. Mulligan declares himself a Nietzschean Übermensch or Superman, a Zarathustra, as he prepares himself for his plunge, in the process finally getting the key from Stephen to hold his clothes down. Stephen turns away, hearing Haines's cheerful "We'll see you again" and thinking of three things proverbially not to be trusted: the "Horn of a bull, hoof of a horse, smile of a Saxon" (732). The young men plan to meet later at The Ship, a public house. Stray phrases of the Latin prayer for the dying accompany Stephen's exit. A circumspect priest finds a niche in which to dress after his swim, but the keyless Stephen has nowhere to go. He will no longer stay in the tower with the night-raving Haines and the capering Mulligan; he cannot go home to his father and sisters. He is as dispossessed as young Telemachus in Homer's epic, who in his father's absence suffered the wasting of his inheritance and the insults of the suitors seeking his mother's hand. Telemachus at least had the goddess Athena (in disguise) to urge him to take courage and search for news about his father. Stephen has had only the old milkwoman. He is a Telemachus in a world which the gods have ceased to visit, and his task will be to learn that he needs a father, not just to search for one.

Surely Stephen knows, and cherishes, the symbolism of his own names—St Stephen, the first Christian martyr, Dedalus, the fabulous artificer (and escapee) of Greek myth. Is he similarly aware of the book's Homeric symbolism, of enacting the role of Telemachus? For that matter is Mulligan, the extravagant admirer of the Greeks, aware of enacting the role of the suitor Antinous, who advises young Telemachus to give up the moody brooding?[1] Apparently not. The characters of Joyce's book go about their business without suspecting the Homeric parallel. After all, none of them has seen the novel's title. At one intriguing moment, much later in the novel in *Scylla and Charybdis* (9.404), Stephen will speak of Shakespeare's character Pericles as "another Ulysses." He is at least aware

---

1. "… let no evil word any more be in thy heart, nor evil work, but let me see thee eat and drink as of old." The *Odyssey* of Homer, tr. S. H. Butcher and A. Lang (London: Macmillan, 1887), pp. 25–26. This is the translation of Homer which Joyce would have read. As A. Walton Litz notes, Joyce also read Charles Lamb's children's version of the *Odyssey*, *The Adventures of Ulysses*, and was influenced by Lamb's symbolic readings of the characters. See *The Art of James Joyce* (London: Oxford University Press, 1961), pp. 1–2.

of the *idea* of Homeric parallels. But perhaps the other important parallel of the chapter does occur to Stephen, as his concluding thought hints: "Usurper." The word applies to Mulligan, of course, who has usurped the key, but also to Claudius in *Hamlet*, who usurped a kingdom. In our young hero, self-pity and a taste for self-aggrandizing literary allusion go hand in hand.

[2] *Nestor* (pages 20–30)

This chapter takes us further from outward event and further into Stephen's mind. What happens—Stephen teaches a history class at Dalkey, a Dublin suburb, and gets paid for his efforts—is less important than what he thinks about the nature of history itself. The texture of the writing thickens with allusions and half-followable associations, all in pursuit of a psychological verisimilitude rarely attempted before *Ulysses*. Joyce moves slowly over a few moments of current time so that his character's speculations may range freely from the mystifying past to the banal present and then to his anxious future.

*   *   *

We begin with Stephen questioning one of his pupils about the battle Pyrrhus fought at Asculum, 279 B.C. This was the original of all "pyrrhic" victories—battles won at such a cost that they essentially become defeats. A later chapter, *Circe*, will demonstrate Stephen's skepticism about the point of all fighting, victorious or otherwise. For now, he is content to extricate a few historical facts from his dullish pupils. Perhaps he thinks of himself as a latter-day Pyrrhus leaning on his spear and "speaking to his officers" (16). Stephen is always highly conscious of the audience for which he is performing. When the daydreaming schoolboy Armstrong takes "Pyrrhus" to mean a pier, Stephen invents a witty definition (a pier, he says, is a disappointed bridge), recalls the possible chapbook of such sayings for Haines, and immediately thinks of himself as a "jester at the court of his master" (44). This is the proper role of Mulligan, one might say, and Stephen worries about having it thrust on him permanently.

He is not a jester with his pupils, but neither is he a very determined teacher. His mind constantly slips away to its own concerns, partly bookish, partly personal. William Blake's writings loom large: at the start of the chapter come quotations and paraphrases from *A Vision of the Last Judgment* and *The Marriage of Heaven and Hell*. These are speculations on the nature of history. Is it a mere pageant of symbols, an allegory fabled by the daughters of memory, or does it have some independent existence? Apocalyptic fragments refer to the future moment when time itself will be fragmented, ruined. Aristotle also appears in paraphrase. Stephen's Catholic education has steeped him in Aristotle and the scholastic philosophers. History is perhaps an Aristotelian "actuality of the possible," a coming-to-be of one event which, "branded" by time, has taken the place of all the other possible events it has precluded (50).

Stephen himself dismisses this airy theorizing as so much weaving of the wind. His pupils want a ghost story. Instead, he has them recite from Milton's "Lycidas" (*"Weep no more, woful shepherds..."*, 64), which gives him respite to recall nights of reading Aristotle in Paris. Milton's references to Christ draw him back to Ireland. The shadow of Christian belief lies on the craven hearts of his pupils and on his own. Christ's riddling answer to the Pharisees' question about paying tribute to Caesar (Mark 12:17) leads to Stephen's own riddle or parable. It is too hard for his pupils to solve, probably by design. In any case the answer to it ("The fox burying his grandmother under a hollybush," 115) does not so much display wit as reveal grief. Stephen cannot put out of mind the mother he has just buried.

Hockey calls all the pupils out but the weakling Cyril Sargent, to whom Stephen gives extra help, reflecting as he does so that a mother once loved this "squashed boneless snail" (142). The riddle is momentarily recalled. Perhaps Stephen would like to be a merciless fox burying, putting out of sight, guilt about loving mothers. The arabic numerals on Sargent's page of addition problems perform a grave morrice dance and suggest the Moorish philosophers who transmitted Aristotle to the West. Thus etymology helps Stephen follow the paths of intellectual history. For him, philosophers like the Moor Averroes or the Jew Maimonides were a "darkness" shining in the "brightness" of Christian Europe—a clever reversal of the language of John 1:5. Cyril Sargent, meanwhile, suggests Stephen himself. "Like him was I" (168). History repeats itself. In a brief, moving passage Stephen acknowledges that part of what he shares with Sargent is loneliness. From this he would be freed.

Stephen waits in the headmaster's study to be paid. There are coins (Caesar) and apostle spoons (Christ), hollow shells, pictures of racehorses—

the dead treasure of the past. The racehorses recall Nestor, whose epithet in the *Odyssey* is "tamer of horses," a garrulous old warrior whom Telemachus visits in hope of news about Ulysses. Mr Deasy is certainly old and garrulous enough to be Nestor—he stands in relation to Stephen as Stephen stood to Sargent—but he is hardly sage enough. This old fogy and Tory of a schoolmaster offers sententious good advice to his young friend. His wise saws about paying his way and being generous but also just and *per vias rectas* ("by straight roads") are the verbal equivalents of his hollow shells. He is a Protestant, an opponent of Irish nationalism, and a misogynist. Like the novelist who created him, Deasy studies historical parallels, as his list of female troublemakers suggests—Eve, Helen of Troy, King Dermod MacMurrough's wife, Kitty O'Shea who brought the great Parnell low[1]— and yet he manages to get some details of history wrong. (It was MacMurrough's mistress, not wife, who provoked the fighting that eventually brought the English King Henry II to Ireland.) Deasy is also, like Haines, an anti-semite.

Stephen responds to the schoolmaster, mentally, by improvising on verbal cues. The mention of the Protestant Orange Lodges generates a paragraph full of imagined Protestant rallying cries culminating in "Croppies [Catholics] lie down" (276), as though Stephen were a walking thesaurus of slogans. Deasy's charge that the Jews "sinned against the light" (361) allows Stephen to re-create a scene on the steps of the Paris stock exchange. Reading this and other imagined vignettes, one can believe that Stephen has artistry in him. Aloud, though, the young man merely seems to match the old man's advice with wise saws of his own. He epigrammatizes himself, producing for Deasy the well-turned phrases he was not willing to produce for Haines: Stephen fears those big words that make them so unhappy (264); history is a nightmare from which he is trying to awake (377).

Meanwhile he receives his pay. Deasy accurately predicts that the three pounds, twelve shillings will not stay long in Stephen's pockets. There follows a brief mental listing of those to whom Stephen owes money. It is

---

1. The great politician Charles Stewart Parnell, the "uncrowned King of Ireland," strove valiantly and effectively for Irish Home Rule. His brilliant career in the English parliament ended when his mistress, Kitty O'Shea, was sued for divorce by her husband; Irish and particularly Catholic sentiment turned against Parnell, who was a Protestant, and he died soon afterwards, repudiated by his own party, a broken man.

hopeless to think of repaying them. In return for his wages Stephen will do the favor of carrying Deasy's letter about foot-and-mouth disease to editors of two papers. (We are given extracts from this letter, a splendid accumulation of clichés.) The favor will make Stephen a "bullock-befriending bard" (431), in Mulligan's opinion and perhaps his own. The chapter ends with a parting shot from Deasy—Ireland has never persecuted the Jews because she never let them in. That claim, as we will see in all the chapters about Leopold Bloom, is doubly wrong.

[3] *Proteus* (pages 31–42)

Possibly Joyce made a tactical error in placing this notoriously difficult chapter so close to the start of the novel. Many a would-be reader of *Ulysses* has slowed at this point, then given up in despair, baffled by Joyce's "obscurantism"—his alleged indulgence in mystery for its own sake. Such a view badly misjudges Joyce. It is important to realize that the chapter's difficulties, however time-consuming, are in no sense gratuitous. They represent the intricacy of Stephen's book-soaked and unhappy mind, and the freedom of his free associations. *Proteus* could not be faithful to Stephen's intellectual heritage without being difficult.

The title points to one of Homer's minor divinities. In the *Odyssey*, Menelaus tells Telemachus of a voyage to Egypt, of being becalmed there, and of a visit to Proteus, the sea god who can assume many shapes but may tell no lies. Menelaus holds fast to Proteus despite rapid transformations and forces the deity to tell him how to continue his voyage. Proteus also has news of Ajax, Agamemnon, and Ulysses. The last is marooned on Calypso's island.

*   *   *

As the chapter begins we accompany Joyce's Telemachus on a walk along Sandymount strand, just south of Dublin and the mouth of the River Liffey. It is late morning, and Stephen savors the changing appearances of external reality. "Ineluctable modality of the visible": that is, "you can't avoid seeing things," but it would not be like Stephen to think so plainly. The unidentified "he" is Aristotle, *maestro di color che sanno*, "master of them that know" as Dante called him, bald but a millionaire and possibly the object of Stephen's envy. After he remembers the Aristotelian theory of the senses, Stephen tries a crude experiment: will the exterior world vanish if he closes his eyes? It does not, he discovers. He walks blind along the beach, listening to his feet (in Mulligan's shoes) crushing wrack and seashells, the solid world fashioned by Blake's demiurge Los (18). Shells make him think of Deasy, who collects them and who has just paid him, though not in "wild sea money." Stephen taps with his ashplant (his stick), sampling the sense of hearing, which is perceived in time (*nacheinander*, "one after the other") rather than, like sight, in space (*nebeneinander*, "next to one another"). The tapping is what the blind ("they") do. Much later, in *Sirens*, a blind man will enter the novel, tapping conspicuously. Tapping leads to rhythm and rhythm to the meter of poetry. Quoting to himself a scrap of verse about Madeleine the mare, Stephen detects in it acatalectic tetrameter "agallop."

This chapter overflows with opposites: seeing and hearing, space and time, the ebb and flow of the tide, random sound and orderly meter, seawrack and seaspawn. One longish sequence of thought begins with the idea of seaspawn, or at least spawn: the generations of humankind. Stephen sees two Dublin frumps coming down to the sea, "our mighty mother." One of them is a midwife, at least in Stephen's fictionalizing mind. Does she have a misbirth to conceal? An infant Moses to hide in the bulrushes (298)? Omphalos, "navel," Mulligan's title for the Martello tower in *Telemachus*, here reassumes its biological meaning. The trailing umbilical cord of birth links Stephen with all previous human generations, all the way back to Adam in "Edenville." Adam, whose telephone number is supplied, may be called on the cable of all flesh. Eve, symbol of beauty but also the womb of sin, tempts Stephen to phrases drawn from Thomas Traherne's meditation on paradise ("orient and immortal," 43), then forces him to consider the dark act of procreation. His own parents formed him in sin. Does that make sinful Stephen share in Simon Dedalus' flesh or his spirit? To use the learned term, is he then "consubstantial" with his father? Stephen wonders where the heretic Arius is, who argued lifelong against the consubstantiality of Father and Son. Stephen's parody word, "con-transmagnificandjewbangtantiality" (51), gathers all aspects of the hoary theological controversy into one portmanteau word and mocks them.

Nipping airs rescue Stephen from the image of Arius' grotesque death in a privy. Mananaan is the Celtic god of the sea, a metamorphosing deity like Proteus. The whole chapter, of course, investigates metamorphosis—

the way seaspawn changes into seawrack, waves into seahorses, Haines and Mulligan into the panthersahib and his pointer (276), actual sight of something on the sand into remembered image of Paris or Dublin.

Stephen, troubled as always by unwelcome obligations, thinks quickly of Deasy's letter, then of a possible visit to his Aunt Sara and Uncle Richie Goulding. Simon Dedalus, Stephen's grandiloquent father, who is quoted by his son as often as Aristotle, would heap scorn on that visit. Simon despises his late wife's family. Yet as Stephen sketches "nuncle Richie" in an imagined or remembered visit, the latter is merely another grand talker in a house of decay. An operatic aria, "*All' erta!*" ("On guard!"), gives Stephen his cue: he must be on his guard against Goulding domesticity (99). Also against Dedalus pride. At Clongowes Wood School the young Stephen boasted of imaginary family connections, but beauty does not lie in ancestry (107) nor in the faded prophecies of Joachim Abbas, who interpreted history as three great ages, of the Father, of the Son, and of the Spirit. Stephen feels closer, as his mind runs on ecclesiastical matters, to the "furious Dean" of St Patrick's Cathedral in Dublin, Jonathan Swift. He ponders the source of prophetic madness, then seems to turn against the idea of priestliness altogether—or against the idea of his own priestliness, one of the infinite Aristotelian possibilities time has ousted. Imagining a priest at a service, Stephen orders "him me" to *Descende, calve*, "come down, bald one, lest you become balder" (113), using Latin because he is paraphrasing Joachim. Priests everywhere are elevating the Host at the same moment. How can God be in each? The English theologian Occam thought of an answer...

But Stephen will never be priest, theologian, or saint. He has prayed too often for naked women. The savage self-examination goes on: his skipping from book to book, his vanity, his authorial fantasies. His epiphanies—his capturings of a moment's essence in prose—were to be sent to all the great libraries of the world. Crackling shells awaken Stephen from this sour reverie. Back to the exterior world for a moment, the world of seawrack now and of human shells. He turns toward the Pigeonhouse (a power-generating station) and recalls lines from Léo Taxil's *La Vie de Jésus*, lighthearted French blasphemy in which Joseph interrogates Mary and learns that it is a pigeon which has put her in her wretched position.

French verse leading naturally enough to the thought of France, we next have a long sequence of Parisian memories, beginning in a café meeting with Patrice Egan, son of the Irish revolutionary exile ("wild

goose") Kevin Egan. The son was skeptical (like Taxil), the father believed
in God. Stephen, meanwhile, was trying to be a student of physics,
chemistry, and natural sciences. He enjoyed the bohemian life of the
Boulevard Saint-Michel but suffered when he arrived too late to cash his
mother's money order at the post office. For a moment Stephen thought of
blasting the French official to bits, then pulled back from violence. "Shake
hands" is ever Stephen's true motto (190), as it is Leopold Bloom's. He was
going to be a wonder-working Irishman on the Continent, like
Columbanus, Fiacre, and Scotus, missionary saints of old (the real saints
laugh from heaven at the pretension), but in actuality he had to retreat
home when he learned of his mother's illness, pretending not to know
English so as not to have to pay the porter.

More images of Paris, some imagined, some recalled. Kevin Egan, now
present in Stephen's memory, sips absinthe ("green fairy," 217) and talks to
Stephen of things Irish, attempting to enlist the young man in the national
cause. "You're your father's son," he says (229), misreading Stephen's
character but contributing to the chapter's debate on consubstantiality.
Egan's gunpowder cigarettes put Stephen in mind of revolutionary
bombings, then of the escape of the Fenian revolutionary James Stephens
from prison in Dublin.[1] Egan once attempted to bomb Clerkenwell Prison
in London and free several Fenians, including Richard Burke, but now he
hides in gay Paree, one of the lost leaders, estranged from wife and son
both. Stephen feels sorry for Egan, who has been forgotten.

Who will clear the breakfast dishes in the Martello tower? Stephen will
not sleep there tonight with Haines and Mulligan. Will he have to walk the
moon's midwatches, like Hamlet? The remaining pages of the chapter draw
frequently on Shakespeare's play. The broody Dane and the broody
Irishman both moralize on human remains (476); Stephen quotes Ophelia
when he thinks of his "cockle hat" and "sandal shoon" (486). The flood
tide is following Stephen, presenting him with a dog's carcass and thoughts
of sand as language, stones as teeth of a giant, "Sir Lout." The giant speaks,
mumbling somewhat. A live dog enters to frighten our hero, who then spies
two figures in the distance. We follow Stephen into the past. Here Vikings
ran their ships up on the strand, here the famished burghers of medieval

---

1. The Fenian Society or Irish Republican Brotherhood, organized in 1858, used
violence to achieve its aim of Irish independence. "You fenians," Deasy says to Stephen in
Nestor (272), using the term loosely perhaps, but still misreading Stephen even more than
Egan does.

Dublin swarmed out to slaughter a school of beached whales. Stephen, in whose veins flows the blood of all past Dubliners, moved among these past lusts and slaughters, among the resin fires on the frozen-over Liffey. But in the past as well as the present he kept his guard up and spoke to no one.

The modern-day dog bays at him and Stephen remembers Mulligan ("primrose doublet," 312), who smiled at Stephen's fear. Mulligan's falsity or Stephen's own pretensions to greatness now make him think of historical Pretenders to thrones, secular heretics, one might say. On his mental list are silken Thomas, Perkin Warbeck, and Lambert Simnel, all famous imposters or false claimants to power in Irish or English history. Those who mock Stephen are like the courtiers in a story by Boccaccio, who do not know they are in their "own house," the graveyard. Stephen cannot quite admit the phrase "House of Death" into his thoughts. Mulligan would not want such medieval "abstruosities" anyway. And yet Mulligan saved a man from drowning. Would Stephen do as much? He would try... He fears water, he does not want to be drowned like Ophelia or the man in Dublin bay. He does not want to be dragged down into guilt about not saving his mother.

Again the dog, who begins, Proteus-like, to take on different appearances, becoming a hare, a buck, a bear, a wolf, a calf, a pard, a panther, a vulture, a fox burying his grandmother in the sand. The recollection of a dream suddenly interrupts Stephen's watching, a dream of a street of harlots and of an oriental man (Haroun al Raschid?) leading him, holding a melon against his face. All this exotic orientalism anticipates what Stephen will experience later with Bloom. (The dream is also Joyce's version of the news Telemachus gets about Ulysses.) Back to the dog and some beachcombing cocklepickers, whom Stephen thinks of as "Egyptians" or gypsies. We are treated to a paragraph full of gypsy cant, and though it seems that Joyce rather than Stephen indulges in this linguistic display, the memory of a gypsy woman in a shawl calling from an archway belongs convincingly enough to the young man. Stephen has embraced ("clipped") and kissed in the "darkmans." Aquinas thought that any dwelling on pleasure—carnal or otherwise—would be a "morose delectation" (385), but the gypsy cant is no worse than Aquinas' Latin. "Roguewords" and "monkwords" are like seawrack and seaspawn, different forms in which reality appears. The cocklepickers pass.

Stray thoughts of a ghost and the flying Dutchman ("pale vampire") give Stephen the words for a poem, which he wishes to "pin down"— record on a scrap of paper. What to use for his tablets? A scrap torn off from Deasy's letter will do, and meanwhile Stephen's mouth plays with sound.[1]

His shadow, as he bends over to write, has an end. But could not his shadow lead endlessly into a mystic world? Stephen might be a soothsayer or augur walking beneath stars unseen in the daylight, "darkness shining in the brightness" (409). But would his endless shadow be his own form? The speculations grow more unconnected and vaporous as Stephen recalls Bishop Berkeley (the "good bishop of Cloyne") and his belief that appearances ("veil of space with coloured emblems") are not aspects of reality but mental creations ("out of his shovel hat," 417). A simile—our souls cling to us as a woman clings to her lover—makes Stephen think of some woman for himself. Perhaps that virgin to whom he gave a keen glance: she would be the dowdy sort who wears suspenders darned with wool, but for all that Stephen longs for her soft touch and the word known to all men, which is "love," as we will later discover.

He relaxes in the sun, brooding no more, gazing on his borrowed boots and remembering another girl in Paris, who admired his small feet. As for Mulligan, he must take Stephen as he is, all or not at all. The waves curl among rocks and speak in their sibilant language to Stephen. Under the tides the seaweeds hold out arms to him and lift their petticoats, and in their weariness at the constant motion (or at Stephen's failure to respond?), they sigh. The drowned man too is somewhere in the water. Characteristically, Stephen ceremonializes him with poetry, "Full fathom five" from Shakespeare's *Tempest* (470), "Sunk though he be" from "Lycidas" (474). But poetry does not prevent Stephen's imagination from making the corpse surface in a horrible seachange that yet becomes part of an endless cycle of Protean metamorphosis.

Stephen thirsts and prepares to leave. For a moment he is in his own estimation the rebel angel Lucifer, who (in the Latin of the Holy Saturday service) is said not to know that he has fallen from heaven. Stephen lunges softly with his ashplant, then recalls a scrap of verse and Alfred Lord Tennyson, a poet and gentleman. Ungentlemanly Stephen is a rebel and a

---

1. In fact the poem is adopted from one of Douglas Hyde's translations from the Gaelic, in *Love Songs of Connaught* (1895). See Gifford and Seidman, p. 62. Does Joyce want us to recognize the source and realize his hero's lack of originality?

poet whose teeth are bad: shells, in fact. Does someone observe the toothless superman putting his nosepickings on a ledge of rock? For all of his Luciferan isolation Stephen must look back once more over his shoulder at the ordinary world which he inhabits, and it is this world, in the form of a threemasted ship, which closes an extraordinary chapter. The *Rosevean* (we later discover the ship's name) is merely carrying bricks, but Joyce, working through Stephen's consciousness, freights it with mystery and beauty as it moves silently upriver, coming home.

[4] *Calypso* (pages 45–57)

Leopold Bloom enters the novel of which he is the hero preparing breakfast for others—the cat, then his wife Molly. His is a life filled with small kindnesses. Also with small defeats and small pleasures: the pork kidney he cooks for his own breakfast is burnt but still toothsome. Bloom will pass through his day thinking of others, enjoying himself, escaping when enjoyment is not possible, suffering when escape is not possible, making do, surviving. He is a middle-aged man of the body (Stephen is a young man of the mind), a married man, and a family man: the Watson to Stephen's Holmes, or the Sancho Panza to the young man's Quixote. The human texture of the novel thickens about Bloom, since he enjoys a wide acquaintance. In his chapters there is less reverie and more action, since he keeps busy. His thoughts—and these Joyce supplies, in quantity—first touch on Dublin and its daily life, then range outward into popular science or the history of his race, making Bloom a fitting counterpart to the great Ulysses, who traveled far and saw the minds of many men. Bloom seeks mental adventures. If his thinking frequently errs, as in his confused notion of black clothes reflecting heat (80), that is merely the equivalent of Ulysses' misadventures among monsters and storms.

When we first glimpse the Homeric Ulysses, indeed, he is mis-adventuring with the amorous nymph Calypso, whose prisoner he has been for seven long years. He longs for his home island Ithaca and his wife Penelope, and to them he is allowed to set sail when Zeus sends Hermes with a message to Calypso: she must let her prisoner go. Joyce's hero, too, first appears to us as a prisoner, of domestic routine, of a small house and a troubled marriage. Molly Bloom is his Calypso. But she is also his Penelope,

the wife for whom he longs and to whom he returns after a brief escape
into the Dublin streets.

*   *   *

In this chapter Joyce returns us to early morning and the awakening of
the Blooms in their house at 7 Eccles Street, Dublin. Bread and butter are
arranged on Molly's tray; the kettle heats on the fire. Greeted by the cat,
Bloom speculates on the feline view of himself (such shifts of perspective
are characteristic of him), on mousing (the masochist in Bloom notes that
mice seem to like cats' cruelty), and on cats' whiskers and the roughness of
their tongues. On his way out to buy a pork kidney, Bloom checks with
Molly, who sighs sleepily in response and turns over, making the loose brass
quoits of the bed jingle. They will jingle throughout the novel. The bed
itself reminds Bloom of Molly's Spanish antecedents—her father, old
Tweedy, was stationed at Gibraltar.[1] Even for a brief journey to the pork
butcher the prudent Bloom takes with him his hat and his lucky potato.
Inside the hat hides a white slip of paper we will learn more about later. The
latchkey Bloom leaves behind, making him the second keyless hero of the
novel.

Out on the street casual observations of the morning scene are
succeeded by a long Eastern reverie. What would it be like to walk along a
strand, pass bazaars inhabited by pantomime "oriental" characters like
Turko the Terrible, meet robbers, hear a mother call her children home?
Bloom's imagined sky is violet, the prose a little purplish. He travels far in
his mind, then comes home with a thought of his Penelope ("colour of
Molly's new garters," 97). Smiling, he pulls himself back from daydreaming.
He is both a sentimentalist and a down-to-earth cynic. Cynically, Bloom
remembers that some images of the sun merely decorate the front page of
newspapers.

Passing the pub of Larry O'Rourke, Bloom considers the benefits to
trade of a new tramline and wonders about all the money made from
pubkeeping in Dublin. No doubt some of the money comes from shady
deals ("a double shuffle," 133). Bloom starts to add up the illicit profits but
is distracted by the noise of schoolchildren. He hears (or imagines?) them at

---

1. The bed did not come from Gibraltar—Molly has misled Bloom about this—but we
do not discover the fact until nearly the end of the novel (*Penelope*, 1214).

a geography lesson in which "Slieve Bloom," an Irish mountain range, is mentioned. But "geography" is metamorphosed into "joggerfry"(139); everyone in this novel, Bloom included, plays with words. Even more distracting than the schoolchildren are sausages in the butcher's window. The servant-girl from the house next door stands ahead of him at the counter. Bloom the voyeur has noticed how her skirt swings when she beats the carpet. Waiting, Bloom peruses a sheet about a Zionist plantation in Palestine. That would suggest that Dlugacz the butcher is Jewish, as Bloom has thought. The cattle pictured on the sheet lead him to think of a previous job he held in the Dublin cattlemarket.

Meat-minded, he is now distracted by the servant-girl's "hams" and wants his kidney in a hurry. Not that he would want to get involved with her: women "never understand" (175). Because he is in a hurry and because he is prudent, Bloom passes up the chance to acknowledge himself as a fellow Jew to Dlugacz, who looks at him eagerly. It will have to be another time. Meanwhile the servant-girl has gone, so Bloom relapses into reading about Agendath Netaim, "the planters' company," and its appeal for investment in Palestine. The idea of quiet long days among the ripening olives or oranges pleases, as does the memory of cool quiet evenings spent years ago with his Jewish friends Mastiansky and Citron, but, as for investing, our cautious hero decides "nothing doing." Thus, ironically, does he answer the call to his Jewish heritage hinted at in the address on the sheet: Bleibtreustrasse, "Remain-true-street."

A cloud covers the sun—the same cloud that shadowed Dublin bay in *Telemachus* and made Stephen think of his mother's death—and turns Bloom gloomy. The Dead Sea, dead names, the oldest people... The weight of history so crushes him that he must shake himself into cheerfulness by an act of will. He ought to do morning exercises and think about practical things, that the house at number twenty-eight remains unrented, for instance. But what really rescues him from gloom is the thought of Molly and her ample bedwarmed flesh. "Yes, yes" (239) sums up Bloom's turn to love and life and, as if to reward him for this turn, sunlight imagined as a girl with gold hair comes running along the street toward him. Thus do the gods always encourage their chosen heroes.

There is a check to joy as Bloom gathers the mail, because Molly has received a letter from Blazes Boylan, her musical impresario and lover. Molly hides this letter away while she reads a postcard from her daughter Milly, who is working in a photographer's shop in Mullingar. Tea is made, the kidney put on the fire. Bloom scans Milly's letter to him. He carries the tray upstairs and questions Molly cautiously about Boylan's letter. He will bring the program for their concert over, she says; she'll be singing *La ci darem* (the seduction duet from Mozart's *Don Giovanni*) and "Love's Old Sweet Song."[1] Part of Joyce's purpose in the novel is to insist that the "dear dead days"—of personal history, of epic adventuring—are never beyond recall. Bloom will attend a funeral at eleven, which is why he is wearing black, like Stephen, but meanwhile Molly wants a word explained. While she hunts for it in her book, *Ruby: the Pride of the Ring*, Bloom wonders if she pronounces the Italian of *La ci darem* correctly ("*Voglio e non vorrei*," 327). Bloom himself does not quite remember the Italian phrase accurately, but its meaning—"I want to and I would not"—might serve as a motto for all the ambivalent characters of *Ulysses*.

Molly's mysterious word is "metempsychosis," the transmigration of souls or reincarnation, needless to say an important concept in a book about a modern-day Ulysses. Bloom explains but gets mixed up with "metamorphosis," being misled by the print of "The Bath of the Nymph" over the bed. He has vaguely recalled stories of Greek nymphs being metamorphosed into trees. But now the smell of burning kidney interrupts the mythological discussion. Bloom dashes downstairs to his slightly scorched breakfast. As he eats he reads Milly's letter with its worryingly casual remarks about a young student who sings Boylan's songs. Will Milly be like Molly? Will sexual history repeat itself? Bloom thinks back to his daughter's birth, then to the birth of his son Rudy, who lived only eleven days. As for Milly, she is vain and wild, but what can Bloom do? It is destiny. It is useless to resist the soft pressure of love. Girls will kiss. Bloom lets the "flowing qualm" (449) of his mingled worry and eroticism spread over him.

The cat wants out and so does Bloom. On his way to the privy he contemplates improvements to the soil and a garden. Full of scraps of

---

1. The first verse of this once-beloved sentimental favorite (words by G. Clifton Bingham, music by James Molloy): "Once in the dear dead days beyond recall, / When on the world the mists began to fall, / Out of the dreams that rose in happy throng, / Low to our hearts, Love sang an old sweet song; / And in the dusk where fell the firelight gleam, / Softly it wove itself into our dream./ Chorus: Just a song at twilight, / When the lights are low / And the flick'ring shadows / Softly come and go; / Though the heart be weary, / Sad the day and long, / Still to us at twilight, / Comes love's old sweet song, / Comes love's old sweet song." For the complete text see Gifford and Seidman, p. 77.

miscellaneous information as always, he recalls that mulch of dung is the best thing to clean ladies' kid gloves. Seated, he passes the time with "Matcham's Masterstroke," from the magazine *Titbits*. A smart piece. Mildly envious, Bloom wonders if he could manage a sketch or a collection of Molly's sayings. The image of Molly dressing leads him to the memory of a dance at which she first met Boylan. She looked into the mirror for wrinkles; Bloom explained the idea behind Ponchielli's *Dance of the Hours*, a famous excerpt from his opera *La Gioconda*. (Ponchielli's gold and gray dancing girls will materialize later in the novel.) Back in the present, Bloom wipes himself with the story he has just been admiring, emerges, checks his black garb in the light, and hears the tolling of the bell of St George's Church.

[5] *Lotus Eaters* (pages 58–71)

Having left Calypso and reached the court of King Alcinous, Homer's Ulysses tells the tale of his wanderings after Troy. An early stop was the land of the lotus-eaters (Egypt?), where three of his men ate the fragrant fruit and lost all desire to return home. Ulysses forced them back to the ships. Joyce's Ulysses does his wandering in midmorning Dublin. Laziness, slow movement, and docility characterize the chapter, which takes Bloom through a few desultory errands as he kills time waiting for the funeral.

* * *

From Sir John Rogerson's quay onward, Bloom's path along the streets can be traced exactly. Joyce took extreme pains to reproduce Dublin in space, and in time as well—the actress Mrs Bandmann Palmer did in fact appear in *Leah* on June 16, 1904, and in *Hamlet* on the previous night, as Bloom recalls (195). At the start of the chapter he moves circuitously toward the Westland Row post office, thinking about Paddy Dignam's funeral. This undertaking job was probably bagged for O'Neill's establishment by Corny Kelleher, whose favorite song refrain Bloom remembers and will keep remembering ("With my tooraloom," 16). Also on his mind is the surreptitious white card hidden in his hat, or "ha" as he tends to think of it. Under the pseudonym "Henry Flower" Bloom is carrying on an affair-by-correspondence with Martha Clifford. At the post office (he might also have used the postal telegraph office, he thinks), he will hand in the card with the name "Henry Flower" on it and see if Martha has sent him anything.

Most of Bloom's musings are stimulated by passing sights, such as the tea packets in a shop window, which suggest Ceylon to him, and leaves to float on, and the Cinghalese (Ceylonese) "not doing a hand's turn all day" (33). This is the first of the chapter's lotus-lands. Even more at ease is a man whom Bloom has seen in a picture, who floats in the Dead Sea and reads a book. Misremembered principles about weight in water and displacement carry Bloom back to classroom physics.

In his last message to Martha, Bloom thinks, he went too far and so can expect no response, but he is wrong. He receives a letter from her and hides it away, awaiting a more secluded spot for its perusal. Recruiting posters on the wall generate some stray thoughts of old Tweedy's regiment and redcoats on the Dublin streets. The eyes of marching soldiers are hypnotized, Bloom thinks (73). He opens Martha's letter while it is still in his pocket but is interrupted by M'Coy, with whom he is forced to exchange a few words. Then the sight of a well-dressed woman on the other side of the street distracts him. When she mounts her carriage she will show Bloom's eager gaze more than just her well-turned foot. Alas, at the crucial moment a heavy tramcar moves between Bloom and the woman. Another interruption. He sighs dully.

M'Coy's tone changes when he asks after Molly. No doubt all of Dublin knows about her affair with Boylan. He squeezes the admission from Bloom that Boylan is "getting up" the forthcoming tour and announces that his own wife, a reedy soprano according to Bloom, has a singing engagement, too. The cautious Bloom thinks immediately that M'Coy is going to ask for the loan of a valise, which will never be returned. He's not to be taken in by that "wheeze." He agrees to put M'Coy's name down as being present at the funeral but resents M'Coy's assumed familiarity ("You and me, don't you know," 185).

As a canvasser or salesman of newspaper advertisements, Bloom always notices advertising. One ad reads:

> *What is home without*
> *Plumtree's Potted Meat?*
> *Incomplete.*
> *With it an abode of bliss.* (143)

These unintentionally obscene phrases will remain with him.[1] A poster advertising Mrs Palmer in *Leah* recalls Bloom's father's fondness for that play, with its climactic scene of the old blind father recognizing the voice of his apostate son. To his own piously Jewish father, Bloom was something of an apostate himself. He thinks briefly, not liking to dwell on the matter, of his father's suicide and of his own preference not to look at the corpse. Like Stephen, though in a less acute way, Bloom would like to bury guilt involving a parent.

Past gelded, docile cabhorses, past a hopscotch court and a child playing marbles, past a watching cat, Bloom seeks a quiet lane for his reading of Martha's letter. She has enclosed a flower for her Henry. She has also made a mistake in her grammar ("my patience are exhausted") as well as the slip of "world" for "word" we have already examined. Bloom's epistolary naughtiness has titillated Martha ("what is the real meaning of that word?"), and twice she says she wishes to punish him. Weak joy opens Bloom's lips as he ponders the language of flowers, the changes in Martha since her first letter, and the prospect of erotic punishment. An actual meeting with Martha? No, thank you, his prudent side responds; no usual love scrimmage for Bloom. An indecent ballad and a painting of Christ in the house of Martha and Mary run companionably together in his mind. He is as drawn as always to quiet coolness and a woman listening with big dark soft eyes. Bloom himself is a man with a Martha and a Mary (Marion, Molly) to talk to.

Barrels of porter bump in his imagination, sending out lotus-flowers over the land, but in action Bloom merely enters All Hallows Church. He considers missionaries, conversion, the Buddha lying at ease on his side. A sodality or association of women at Mass are receiving their lotus-flower. Bloom listens to the stupefying Latin and observes an old fellow asleep, safe in his blind faith. I. N. R. I. on the priest's vestment? To Bloom this is not *Iesus Nazarenus Rex Iudaeorum* but "iron nails ran in." The nails match the thorns in roses and pins in ladies' clothes he has thought about earlier. Following his wife's lead, Bloom interprets I. H. S. as "I have sinned" (his own guilt revealing itself?), then as "I have suffered" (his masochism?). Molly once sang in a different church, calling to mind sacred composers, chanting monks and liqueurs, and eunuchs in the choir. Eunuchdom is one

---

1. "To pot meat" is to engage in sexual intercourse.

way out of the sexual fray, Bloom observes. He also notes that everyone
wants confession: "Punish me, please" (426).

Exit Bloom, buttoning his trouserfly and thinking of forbidden
glimpses. He is off to the chemist (druggist) Sweny to have a lotion made
up for Molly. Drugs, too, are an anodyne. There will be time before the
funeral for a Turkish bath; Bloom buys soap. Bantam Lyons holds him for
a moment with a request to look at Bloom's rolled-up copy of the *Freeman's
Journal*. Lyons is looking for a hot tip on the Gold Cup race to be run at
Ascot this day, and he thinks he's got one when Bloom tells him to keep
the paper, since he was just about to throw it away. "Throwaway," we will
discover, is a horse running in the race. Not knowing what he has provided,
Bloom wanders innocently away, smiling at the silliness of gambling and
recalling one young wastrel who will never come back from America—the
"Fleshpots of Egypt" (548). There is one "Damn bad ad" to notice, and
then Bloom imagines greeting the porter Hornblower at the gate of Trinity
College, so that one day he might go in and enjoy the cricket. Thus he is
always "working," or thinking of "working," someone else for small favors.

The current heat wave will not last, suggesting to Bloom the stream of
life always passing by, suggesting the words of an operatic aria drawled out
in his memory ("dearer thaaan them all," 564), suggesting finally the bath,
which he foresees as a "mosque" because it is Turkish, but also because this
morning his mind has been fascinated by the East. Bloom shows no sign of
Stephen's dislike of cleansing waters. In the bath he will recline at ease,
washed and scented, his "limp father of thousands" metamorphosed into a
floating lotus flower.

[6] *Hades* (pages 72–95)

"Are we all here now?" Martin Cunningham asks his fellow mourners
as they enter the carriage conveying them to Paddy Dignam's funeral. Then,
in an afterthought, "Come along, Bloom" (8). Throughout the chapter
Joyce's hero will be subtly snubbed. Indeed, he will be subtly snubbed
throughout the novel and on occasion openly derided. Bloom does not
belong to the crowd of nominally Christian and casually anti-semitic
Dubliners with whom he associates and, moreover, is temperate when they
are indulgent (in alcohol, in sentiment), purposeful when they are at ease,
curious when they are close-minded. And yet he cannot, Dublin being the

small city it is, disappear into anonymity. He must constantly participate in civic life, as he participates in this funeral, must expose himself to censure or worse.

Past opened drains and ripped-up streets and over the canals of the city the mourners' carriage goes. This is, after all, Joyce's version of the epic hero's descent to the underworld, to the rivers of Hades which must be crossed if the hero is to speak to the shades of fallen comrades and gain the knowledge necessary for the rest of the journey. In the *Odyssey*, Agamemnon, murdered by his wife Clytemnestra, warns Ulysses that no woman is to be trusted, while Achilles inquires eagerly after his son and while Ajax, Ulysses' former rival for the armor of Achilles, stalks off angrily. Joyce contrives equivalents for all these figures, but the more important Homeric parallel in the chapter is its atmosphere, its absorption into the horrors of the grave. Dublin is thronged this June morning with people wearing black. As the mourners proceed to Prospect Cemetery in Glasnevin and Paddy's grave, Death's dominion seems to expand uncontrollably, and it will be Bloom's mental task to limit it.

* * *

At the start he merely wants to be treated companionably. Politely, he allows Simon Dedalus to enter the carriage first, then makes himself helpful by pointing out Stephen. (Has the young man's mourning caught Bloom's eye?) All he gets in return is a joyless smile. Simon thinks Stephen corrupted by a lowdown crowd. Achilles-like, he is fascinated by his son, as Bloom would be by Rudy if he had lived. Lapsing into paternal sentimentality, Bloom imagines teaching his son German. He can remember the morning Rudy was conceived ("How life begins," 81). "Life, life" (90) is our advertising man's phrase for the not-unpleasant helplessness he feels in contemplating all irrevocable natural processes: Rudy's dying, Milly's growing up to be like her mother.

Later this evening, should Bloom see *Leah* or *Fun on the Bristol?* Music, songs...*her* songs. Boylan is coming to visit Molly this afternoon, and no sooner does Bloom's rival come to mind than he appears on the street, doffing his hat. This is an example of a curious and repeated phenomenon of *Ulysses*: the seeming power of thoughts to engender action—one might say, the opposite of interior monologue, in which action engenders thought. With Boylan in sight, Bloom immediately attempts mental discipline ("My

nails. I am just looking at them," 204). Sly questions about the concert tour
follow. Bloom will not accompany the tour himself because he will be in
Ennis, County Clare, visiting his father's grave on the anniversary of his
suicide, a death much in his thoughts this day.

The well-known Dublin moneylender Reuben J. Dodd is hobbling
along the street. All have been to see him—all but Bloom the Jew, that is—
and as if to prove himself a regular fellow Bloom plunges into an anecdote
about Reuben J. and his son, only to be rudely interrupted by Martin
Cunningham. All laugh, then decide they had better look serious for
Paddy's sake. It was a sudden death, they remark; the best death, Bloom
adds, not having a Catholic's concern about deathbed repentance. The
conversation turns to the cowardice of suicide. Bloom remembers phrases
from his father's suicide letter. To counter gloom he mentions the
municipal funeral trams used in Milan and, ever curious, asks himself if
corpses bleed when cut. Gloomy gardens pass, then the house of a murder
victim. The carriage is at its destination in the northwest quadrant of Dublin
(Ulysses also travels to the northwest to find Death's kingdom: here one
hero's voyage is mapped onto the other's with particular exactitude).[1]
Paddy Dignam has arrived before his mourners, like the dead Elpenor in
the *Odyssey*, who reaches the underworld before Ulysses. (There is still
another link between the two: Elpenor fell off Circe's rooftop when drunk,
and Paddy's downfall, as we learn from his friends, was "Liquor…Many a
good man's fault," 572).

Martin Cunningham is going to "get up a whip" (collect money) for the
Dignam children (564); we will hear of Bloom's contribution later. Now he
wonders if an undertaker's horse knows what it draws to the cemetery, then
meditates on a different burden, widowhood, and the futility of mourning.
What matters is "Something new to hope for" (553), but then it is also true
that someone must go first into death, lie alone in the ground. Here and
elsewhere in the chapter Bloom's faith in continuing life does battle with a
fascinated disgust at death. As for the promise of Christian immortality,
Bloom feels detached, even cynical about that. The Latin funeral service,
which he follows from a non-committal position at the back, asks the Lord
not to enter into judgment with His servant (601) and to defend sinners
against temptation (618), but to Bloom this is only so much

---

1. Michael Seidel, *Epic Geography: James Joyce's Ulysses* (Princeton: Princeton University
Press, 1976), pp. 34–35. Seidel's study investigates many geographic parallels between
Homer and Joyce.

"Dominenamine" (594). He stays controlled when the others sentimentalize at the monument of "the Liberator," Daniel O'Connell, and when with facile Irish emotionalism Simon Dedalus weeps at the thought of his wife's recent death. On the way to the grave Bloom brings up the rear with the other odd-man-out, the Protestant Kernan, but resists the latter's piety. "I am the resurrection and the life" may be all very well, but the Bloomian creed is "Once you are dead you are dead" (677).

John O'Connell, the caretaker of the cemetery and thus Joyce's equivalent of Hades himself, the god of the underworld, tactfully distracts the mourners from their grief with a joke about drunks among the tombstones. In Bloom's mind this leads to thoughts about other forms of life in the midst of death: sex, for example. Are women repelled or excited by "courting death," romancing among the graves? Lovemaking would certainly be tantalizing for the onlookers, the dead in their coffins. Bloom interests himself in the perspective even of the buried. And in the uses of the buried. If graveyards are gardens, then corpses are potential fertilizer for the cycle of life. Bloom concocts a ghoulish ad for the well-preserved corpse of an epicure.

He notes that rarity in Dublin, a complete stranger, a man in a macintosh. Bloom would like to know who he is but never finds out (nor does the reader). "If we were all suddenly somebody else" (836), Bloom wonders. The phrase comes from nowhere and leads to nothing, but it is a fitting motto for his sympathetic curiosity. Next he sympathetically thinks himself into the position of a corpse. What if you were buried prematurely? To exorcise this horrible idea Bloom thinks ingeniously of coffins with airholes and warning devices. Hynes takes names for the newspaper account of the funeral; the gravediggers are tipped. It would be more sensible to spend money on the living, but in contradiction to this seeming callousness Bloom is soon anticipating his next visit to his father's grave. He will pay the gardener ten shillings to keep the grave free of weeds.

On their way out the funeral party passes the grave of Charles Stewart Parnell, the Irish Agamemnon. An emblem of the Sacred Heart draws from Bloom some confused memories of a Greek painting of fruit so realistic it attracted birds. Then an obese grey rat scuttles by. Where is it going? With mounting horror Bloom imagines the "Regular square feed" the rats get from the dead, the "Saltwhite crumbling mush" of decayed flesh (994). There are even those who open graves to get at fresh buried females. Bloom has clearly had enough of the place. The mood is getting him down;

ghosts are threatening. Suddenly Bloom recalls Martha's mistaken phrase about not liking that other "world." Nor does he like the other world of death. In a decisive act of mental heroism Bloom acknowledges that there is plenty for him to see and hear and feel yet (1003). Like all the epic heroes who have preceded him, Bloom draws wisdom from but is not conquered by Hades' realm. He shakes off his gruesome mood and leaves thinking of warm fullblooded life. Still, he is snubbed on his way out, by the Ajax-figure John Henry Menton, who cannot forgive Bloom for besting him at lawn bowling or Molly for marrying Bloom. Even at its most heroic moments, our Ulysses' life is filled with minor defeats, insults, kindnesses refused.

[7] *Aeolus* (pages 96–123)

Repartee, bombast, puns, flowers of rhetoric, and other forms of journalistic hot air abound in this chapter, which is set in the offices of the *Evening Telegraph* and *Freeman's Journal*, for which Bloom works as a salesman ("canvasser") of advertisements. Dublin's newspapermen and their hangers-on entertain each other with riddles and parodies, quote limericks and famous orations, and in general wholly disregard Professor MacHugh's warning that they "mustn't be led away by words, by sounds of words" (485). Joyce, a little led away by words himself, decorates the narrative with rhetorical devices such as asyndeton, the deliberate omission of conjunctions, as in "They watched the knees, legs, boots vanish" (63), or chiasmus, the repetition of matched phrases in inverted order, as in the wonderful pair of sentences about grossbooted draymen rolling barrels dullthudding (21) already quoted. Most obviously, Joyce punctuates the chapter with newspaper headlines in capital letters. Bloom and Red Murray appear under the words "GENTLEMEN OF THE PRESS," a euphemism, while "THE CROZIER AND THE PEN" (61) is a synecdoche (part taken for whole) and "O, HARP EOLIAN!" (370) is an apostrophe (direct address). These headlines befit the world of a newspaper office, of course, but what happens to them does not. They begin in a ponderous late nineteenth-century style but grow more exclamatory ("OMINOUS—FOR HIM!", 871) and finally tabloidish. They evolve, that is, as if to demonstrate that journalistic prose has a life of its own, apart from the will of human beings. Meanwhile the human beings in *Aeolus* from start to finish accomplish nothing and remain their feckless if eloquent selves. For the first time in

Ulysses, Joyce here treats language as something with a life apart from character and setting.

*   *   *

Joyce conducts us to the noisy center of Dublin and the equally noisy newspaper offices, full of swishing doors and thumpings of the press. Bloom picks up a copy of an old ad for the wine merchant Alexander Keyes and observes, with Red Murray, the stately entrance of William Brayden, who looks like Christ, or like the tenor Giovanni Mario. The tenor makes Bloom think of the aria "When first I saw that form endearing" from Flotow's opera *Martha*, a recollection preparing the way for important doings later. On his way to the printing foreman (and Member of Parliament and Dublin City Councillor) Nannetti, Bloom recalls Dignam's funeral, then hints that Hynes might repay what he owes him. No luck. But Nannetti will approve the ad and a plug for Keyes' business, "a little par calling attention" (156), if Bloom can get Keyes to renew the ad for three months. The crossed-keys design wanted for the ad Bloom will copy from a Kilkenny paper. This advertising emblem hints at a novelistic structure: the paths of our two keyless heroes, Bloom and Stephen, will cross momentarily in this episode.

Through the case room Bloom proceeds, watching type being set backwards, remembering his father reading Hebrew from right to left, misremembering Passover chants. "[I]nto the house of bondage" (209) should be "out of the house of bondage," of course, but Bloom's unconscious mind knows some forms of bondage are inescapable— perhaps even desirable. Molly's soap is transferred to his hip pocket. Should he go home to see her dress? No, he decides (231). Softly (Bloom likes an unobtrusive entrance) he goes into an office where Ned Lambert, Simon Dedalus, and Professor MacHugh are making fun of Dan Dawson's empurpled speech about the lovely land of Ireland. Soon, in comes J. J. O'Molloy, a gambler and mighthavebeen now "Reaping the whirlwind" (304) of his misdeeds. (As we would expect in a chapter named after the guardian of the winds, Joyce provides much metaphorical breeziness to go along with the literal draftiness in the newspaper offices.) Lambert quotes more of Dawson's oratory until Simon Dedalus protests and calls for a drink. Myles Crawford, the editor, comes out of his inner office, apoplectically, and Bloom goes in to use the telephone. Lenehan hears the "feetstoops" of newsboys rushing in, thus contributing a playful metathesis or reversal of letters to the rhetorical display. Later Lenehan will reverse the consonants in "Damn clever" to produce "Clamn dever" (695). Meanwhile we overhear bits of Bloom's telephone call to Keyes. Bloom will have to track his man down at Dillon's auction rooms; capering newsboys follow him down the street, imitating his walk.

A sponge, and a jester like Mulligan, Lenehan earns a cigarette by being prompt with a match. Ineffectual like everyone else in the chapter, he has trouble squeezing a riddle in as first Professor MacHugh casts scorn on so-called Roman civilization and then O. Madden Burke enters with Stephen, gracefully allegorizing ("Youth led by Experience visits Notoriety," 508). Lenehan finally manages to ask what opera resembles a railway line while Stephen presents Mr Deasy's letter about hoof-and-mouth disease. It is now a torn letter because Stephen has used part of it for his poem about the "pale vampire." The professor celebrates more lost causes, mentioning Pyrrhus again, and then the Greek intellect; Lenehan whispers a limerick and finally gives the answer to his riddle: *The Rose of Castile*. Burke feigns a "strong weakness" (594), indulging in oxymoron or contradiction. At the mention of Molly Bloom, Lenehan insinuates a phrase about her alleged wantonness ("The gate was open," 613) which only becomes clear later, in *Wandering Rocks*.

In the meantime Crawford encourages Stephen, holding up the example of the journalist Ignatius Gallaher and his famous scoop about the Phoenix Park murders (Gallaher cabled the escape route to New York in code).[1] The appeal to his youthful ambition reminds Stephen of Father Dolan's accusing words to him ("See it in your face," 618), as recorded in *A Portrait of the Artist as a Young Man*.

Bloom telephones but is rudely ignored amid all the talk of the old journalists, the old silvertongued orators, while Stephen ponders rhyming words from various passages in Dante. To him, the Italian triple rhymes suggest threesomes of approaching girls (720). Stephen is always drawn to girlish beauty, always capable of detachment from his immediate surroundings, and always self-conscious. In a moment, he will wonder what someone has said about him. O'Molloy quotes Seymour Bushe orating in the Childs murder case while Stephen seems to think of recording the

---

1. In 1882 a group of Irish revolutionaries (the "Invincibles") assassinated two English officials in Phoenix Park, Dublin.

moment in all-too-novelistic prose ("I have often thought...," 763). Then MacHugh quotes John F. Taylor speaking of the outlaw Moses at the college historical society. This oration, like *Ulysses* itself, shows how the present may be read in the past, how Hebrews and Irishmen have alike been subjected to great empires.

The Hebrew Irishman Bloom is not present to hear the speech, but Stephen seems challenged by it ("Could you try your hand at it yourself?," 836). A little later, recalling Daniel O'Connell's protest meetings at Tara and Mullaghmast and the words "Gone with the wind" (880), he contemplates the pointlessness of speechmaking and suggests a drink at Mooney's. Before they all leave, O'Molloy takes the editor aside to ask for a loan. Stephen would not perform for Haines earlier, but now he entertains the thirsty journalists with a story about two old women climbing Nelson's pillar, a famous Dublin monument which we saw briefly at the beginning of the episode. Perhaps the newsboys' cry "Racing special!" (914) has provoked him into creating something special out of the ordinary Dublin life surrounding him. Stephen's slice-of-life realism in this odd tale, "*A Pisgah Sight of Palestine* or *The Parable of The Plums*," is probably meant to contrast with all the rhetoric of the chapter. Certainly it contrasts with the slangy virtuosity of the headlines, which are now at their wildest. Stephen's title, meanwhile, provides yet another link between the Hebrews and the Irish; it reaches back over the centuries to recall Moses, who from the top of Mount Pisgah achieved the sight of the Promised Land, only to die soon thereafter. Stephen's Anne Kearns and Florence MacCabe want to see views of Dublin but are too tired to look down.

Bloom enters for the last time, full of what Keyes wants about the ad; the editor snubs him again. For a moment Bloom wonders protectively about young Dedalus, and then after a few more verbal flourishes, this chapter of disappointments comes to an end. Bloom fails to get his money back from Hynes or impress anyone with the urgency of his business; O'Molloy gets no loan; Stephen's story trails off somewhat pointlessly ("Finished?" Miles Crawford asks, 1031). All these failures correspond to a last-minute disaster in Ulysses' homecoming. King Aeolus gives the hero a bag of captured storm winds to ensure a calm voyage, but just before the ship reaches Ithaca, Ulysses' men, thinking they will find booty, open the bag and release a tempest. "Look out for squalls" (983) must remain the motto of Ulysses and Bloom alike.

[8] *Lestrygonians* (pages 124–150)

From the rhetorical performances of the previous episode we proceed
to solider concerns, above all, food, as Bloom and most of Dublin move
toward lunch. Bloom moves rather slowly, passing judgment on such items
as scoopfuls of creams and phosphorescent codfish, remembering Molly's
tastes when pregnant, and enjoying the sights of a Dublin which seems bent
on making him hungry (the chapter supplies dozens of punning phrases
about food, including "Graham Lemon's," "sandwichmen," "oyster eyes
staring at the postcard," "the reverend Dr Salmon"). In the *Odyssey* Ulysses,
too, is hungry. He and his men visit the land of the Lestrygonians, who turn
out to be giants and cannibals. Only Ulysses and the crew of his own ship
escape being killed and eaten.

* * *

For a moment Bloom thinks he sees his name on a street throwaway
(he is always alert to the mention of his name) but then realizes the sheet is
touting the blood of the lamb. All are welcome to a revival meeting. This is
a "Paying game," Bloom the skeptic thinks. Spying Dilly Dedalus, Stephen's
sister, he meditates on big Catholic families and priests living off the fat of
the land, then sympathizes with an underfed child and hungry gulls.
Charitable as ever, he feeds the gulls cake. A sign floating on the river
prompts thoughts of advertising. A quack doctor once stuck up notices
about treatment for the clap in Dublin's outdoor privies. In a sequence of
worried phrases which he is barely able to admit to his consciousness,
Bloom wonders if Blazes Boylan might have "a dose" of the clap himself
("If he ....?", 102).
Quickly Bloom turns his attention to the time and the astronomical
term "parallax," a Greek word to go with "metempsychosis," which he
remembers in Molly's mispronunciation. "Parallax"—the apparent shift in a
celestial object's position, when seen from different perspectives—hints at
Joyce's shifts in narrative perspective and at his ability to see characters and
situations in their full roundedness. All this will later become clear; for now,
Bloom shifts back to speculations on advertising. Sandwichmen with their
notice boards for Wisdom Hely's, the stationer, don't bring in business.
That sort of advertising is nearly as bad as a notice for Plumtree's potted
meat under the obituaries. When Bloom worked for Wisdom Hely, he

proposed using a transparent show cart with smart office girls inside, thus appealing to everyone's curiosity and to his own voyeurism.

Next we have miscellaneous thoughts about nuns and the Blooms' past ("Happy. Happier then," 170). Sentimentally Bloom recalls cooking mutton for Molly's supper and sitting on the bed warmed by her body. Suddenly his old acquaintance Mrs Breen turns up, telling a tale of woe about her dotty husband, who has received an insulting postcard. "U.p: up" (258) means something like "it's all up with you," and hints at some obscure sexual disorder as well, with its nasty insinuation that Breen "pees up." More arcanely, the initials hint at Ulysses and Penelope. With pity Bloom hears of Mina Purefoy in the maternity hospital, who is laboring to bring forth life. She is the biological analogue to Philip Beaufoy, who brought forth "Matcham's Masterstroke" (one reason Bloom confuses the names?). With a smile he watches the grandiloquently named Farrell, a well-known street eccentric. On past the *Irish Times*, where there might be other answers to the ad ("Wanted, smart lady typist...," 326) which Martha and forty-three others answered. Bloom imagines the newspaper's "toady" references to the English vicereine, the foxhunting news in the *Irish Field*, and aristocratic women. He is fascinated by mannish, "horsey" types.

The sight of wellfed policemen marching by recalls a student riot, when Bloom was nearly chased down by a mounted policeman but in compensation got to know Dixon, a young doctor—another surrogate son, perhaps. He thinks of plainclothesmen wheedling information out of "slaveys," servant girls. Young political hotheads may believe that "great times" are coming, but all political rant is for Bloom useless verbiage, because "Things go on same" (477). A heavy cloud produces a melancholy sense of flux: children keep being born, houses keep changing hands. The sun comes out and Charles Stewart Parnell's brother passes, then the poet George Russell ("A.E.") with a woman disciple, talking occult symbolism. Perhaps the loose-stockinged young woman is Lizzie Twigg, who responded to Bloom's ad (330). Mysticism and vegetarianism do not appeal to him, but science does. Perhaps he could go to the observatory someday and ask the professor about parallax. But he would need to be polite ("Cap in hand," 577). Thoughts of the moon lead to Molly and to Boylan ("He"). Bloom tries to discipline himself ("Stop. Stop," 592) but can't help recalling the past: after Rudy's death, he could never like sex with Molly.[1] To bolster his self-esteem, he reminds himself of Martha Clifford and the letter he must write to her. Full of vague longing for womankind, imagining a world full of lovemaking, Bloom finally reaches the Burton restaurant, but there men are wolfing down their food like animals or like the cannibal Lestrygonians of the *Odyssey* ("Eat or be eaten," 703). Bloom is sickened. In reaction to thoughts of Boylan, that very masculine man, he is also disgusted by male smells. Some utopian day, perhaps, hunger will be assuaged by communal kitchens or by "tabloids" (food tablets), but for now Bloom will seek a sandwich in Davy Byrne's genteel pub.

There, at the bar, he greets Nosey Flynn and orders a glass of burgundy and—in spite of what he has just thought about vegetarianism—a cheese sandwich. He recalls a dirty limerick about eating and, while on the subject of food, the fast of Yom Kippur. For a second time Bloom is asked "Who's getting up" Molly's concert tour; unconsciously defending his masculinity, perhaps, he remembers the rest of the limerick. Byrne enters and is interrogated about the Gold Cup race, but Bloom, who has a bit of the artist about him, as we will later hear, takes more interest in the curve of wood in the bar. The "Mild fire" of the wine leads to a long meditation on odd food tastes, oysters (a reputed aphrodisiac), waiters in swell hotels, and the rich fishmonger Micky Hanlon. But Bloom cannot forget Molly for long, and he savors the memory of making love to her on Howth Head under the wild ferns. "Me. And me now," he thinks (917), contrasting his past and present selves as Stephen has done before and will continue to do in the next chapter.

When Bloom leaves to urinate, Byrne asks about him. Nosey Flynn thinks he gets money from fellow Masons ("the craft," 960) and doesn't like to drink. Newcomers to the bar continue giving misinformation about our hero, as Bantam Lyons hints that he has gotten his Gold Cup tip (Throwaway) from Bloom. Meanwhile the alleged tipster is on his way to the National Library to look up the Kilkenny ad that he needs. There, pretending to drop something, he will be able to examine the statues of goddesses (931). Do they have a hole behind like humans? (In its mixture of prurience and quasi-scientific curiosity this is a quintessentially Bloomian

---

1. "Could never like it again ..." (610) has no grammatical subject and so leaves open the possibility that *Molly* has turned away from sex with her husband, or the possibility that Bloom *assumes* she has turned away.

inquiry.) On the street he hums music from Mozart's *Don Giovanni*, adds up money coming in, and contemplates buying a petticoat for Molly. After generosity, kindness; he helps a blind stripling cross the street. Will he send a postal order to Martha—the "mistress" he has never seen? More immediately, he wants to feel his belly skin, to test the theory that colors have different feels. This is an experiment in sensation to balance Stephen's closed eyes on Sandymount strand. How sad that anyone should be blind, Bloom thinks; how distressing that so many people should be drowned on an excursion in New York (a news item that will keep cropping up through the day).

At the library, after so much thinking about him, Bloom encounters Boylan, identified as usual by his straw hat, tan shoes, and turned-up (i.e., cuffed, and therefore fashionable) trousers. Panicking, Bloom flees to the museum, where he will take refuge in esthetic concerns—a handsomely designed building, "curves of stone" (1180)—just as earlier he took refuge in Davy Byrne's pub, with its curved oaken bar. He hides his agitation in a pretended search of his pockets, then reaches the gate and is, as the last word of the episode emphasizes, "Safe!": safe from Boylan, who might see and despise him, safe from his own beating heart and disquiet.

[9] *Scylla and Charybdis* (pages 151–179)

Whereas Bloom remembers proverbs, popular songs, and scraps of scientific information, Stephen remembers esoteric phrases and scraps of literature. Through his day the young man goes, *"reading the book of himself"* like the Hamlet of Mallarmé's poem (115), and remembering all the other books which have formed him. Nowhere is Stephen's erudition on clearer or more appropriate display than in the National Library, where amid volumes of accumulated knowledge, "Coffined thoughts" (352), a few Irish literati listen skeptically to the young man's theories about Shakespeare and eagerly drop quotations themselves. None of the participants in the discussion can escape the grip of literature. Even their movements seem to be ruled by what they have read. Hence the dance terms at the beginning of the chapter, "sinkapace" and "corantoed," which are quoted from Shakespeare, the first of an extraordinary number of quotations from or allusions to the Bard of Avon. Later, under the influence of so much talk about plays and players, the episode will momentarily assume dramatic form, with speech prefixes and stage directions. Bookishness and a sort of intellectual cattiness affect the very narration of the chapter.

All the learned allusiveness makes *Scylla and Charybdis* difficult. The first two pages alone mention or quote Goethe (whose character Wilhelm Meister translates *Hamlet*), Matthew Arnold on Shelley ("beautiful ineffectual dreamer"), John Milton, Marie Corelli (author of the bestselling *The Sorrows of Satan*), W. B. Yeats's "A Cradle Song" (the "shining seven"), Dante, John Synge (*In the Shadow of the Glen*), Ben Jonson, Plato, and Aristotle. The two Greek philosophers represent extremes of beautiful ineffectual dreaming and hard merciless logic. Between these Stephen must steer, and between other extremes (such as believing in his *Hamlet* theory and not believing it), just as Ulysses had to avoid both the many-headed, snapping monster Scylla and the dizzying whirlpool Charybdis by steering between them. At this point in the novel, then, Stephen temporarily drops the role of Telemachus to assume that of Ulysses. Like Bloom, he becomes a mental mariner.

As for Stephen's theory, it is based on an assumption nowhere explicitly stated—that literature is inescapably autobiographical, being created out of the turbulences of private life, out of the writer's personal longings, resentments, or guilts. "We walk through ourselves," Stephen will argue, "always meeting ourselves" (1044). Walking through his turbulent family life, Shakespeare created characters who were versions of himself or of those close to him. But he did not make Prince Hamlet a version of himself as so many have argued. Instead, Stephen theorizes, Shakespeare re-created himself as the ghost of Hamlet's father (here Stephen relies on the old theatrical tradition that the actor Shakespeare played this very part).[1] Why should Shakespeare identify himself with the ghostly, betrayed father? The answer is that he was betrayed himself. His wife at home in Stratford, Ann Hathaway, committed adultery with his brothers Edmund and Richard; Ann became the guilty Queen Gertrude of *Hamlet*, his brothers the usurping King Claudius (they also became the villains of *Richard III* and *King Lear*). Meanwhile Shakespeare's son Hamnet died at age eleven (Bloom's son Rudy, we must recall, died at eleven days), and the lost son in real life became the son onstage; Hamnet became Hamlet. Shakespeare achieved a measure of serenity only in old age, when his daughter Susanna bore a

---

1. In *Lestrygonians* (8.67) Bloom has quoted to himself lines spoken by Hamlet's father.

daughter, who became Miranda, Perdita, Marina, the lost-then-recovered heroines of the last romances.

* * *

At the start of the episode, it is 2 o'clock and Stephen is in the midst of discussion with Thomas Lyster, the Quaker librarian of the National Library, "John Eglinton" (W. K. McGee, an Irish man of letters and assistant librarian), and A.E. (George Russell, the well-known poet and mystic, who sits somewhat apart from the others, in shadow). An attendant calls Lyster out to business. A.E. dismisses biographical speculations about Shakespeare, preferring instead "eternal wisdom, Plato's world of ideas" (52), and Stephen mockingly contemplates theosophy, the particular form of wisdom to which A. E. is devoted. If the phrases moving through Stephen's mind ("the sacrificial butter," "moisture of light," "repentant sophia") are hard to decipher, that is partly because the theosophists' "life esoteric is not for ordinary person" (69). In a moment Stephen, no deliberate mystifier, will labor to clarify his own theory for the ordinary persons listening to him.

Richard Best, another assistant librarian, enters, remarking that he has just shown Jubainville's book on Celtic myth to the Englishman Haines. While Stephen recalls their breakfast-time encounter, A. E. distinguishes between visionary peasant hearts and sophisticated literary corruption, as seen in Mallarmé, whose poem serves to bring the discourse back to *Hamlet*. The play ends in a bloodbath, Stephen says, as though its hero were a Hamlet wearing khaki uniform from the just-fought Boer War. He shifts to a description of the Globe theatre on a midafternoon in June, working in all the "Local colour" (158) he can. That is, he exercises himself in what the Jesuits call "Composition of place," praying appropriately to Ignatius Loyola as he does so (163). Shakespeare enters onstage, playing the ghost, wearing a courtier's discarded armor; Joyce's phrase "court buck" (165) hints at the clothes which Stephen himself has borrowed from Buck Mulligan. It is not, after all, surprising that Stephen should be like Shakespeare. Are not Stephen's writings as autobiographical as Shakespeare's? Does not "corrupt Paris" lie as far from Dublin as London lies from Stratford (149)? Proceeding with his theory, Stephen identifies Hamlet with Hamnet, the guilty queen with Ann Hathaway; after A. E. objects, Stephen remembers, in a little argument with himself, that he owes

A. E. a pound. Even the thinking is dialectic, full of give-and-take, in this episode.

Next, Stephen derives the tortured sexuality of the narrative poem *Venus and Adonis* from Shakespeare's memories of being seduced, tumbled in a cornfield, by his wife to be. "And my turn?" the young man asks himself in a moment of self-pity (261). In his role as bullockbefriending bard, he proffers Deasy's letter to A. E., but not before defending himself by satirical contemplation of theosophy. At a meeting this evening the work of young Irish poets will be read. From this sort of literary career-making Stephen is excluded, as the word "Nookshotten" (315), "pushed into a corner," suggests. A. E. departs and Lyster re-enters, making Stephen identify Shakespeare with George Fox, the founder of Quakerism, and then in response to further questions, Stephen fashions an important statement about the artist weaving and reweaving his image (376). With the aid of such imaginative transformations, the past may create the future, the father create the son. But in a sense the future also creates the past. The Stephen of future days will see himself as he sits here now, but in a changed way, because he will be changed himself (384). In other words, perspectives shift as the years go by; a parallax in time matches the parallax in space Bloom has been wondering about. As for reconciliation, that is indeed the subject of Shakespeare's last plays. In his love for the young heroines like Miranda, the playwright recovers his lost love for Ann Hathaway. The word known to all men (and known finally to all readers of *Ulysses*, thanks to the new edition), is "Love" (429).[1]

There follows a long speculation on Shakespeare's sexual disillusion. According to Stephen, the playwright's belief in himself was "untimely killed" when he was seduced by Ann Hathaway, and a new passion followed, the tortured love for the dark lady of the sonnets. At the height of Stephen's eloquence, in a theatrically striking entrance, Buck Mulligan comes in, mocking Stephen as usual, and producing in Stephen a mock-Creed, a Creed as if declaimed by heretics. For a while Best and Eglinton carry on with the Shakespearean discussion, trying to explain the puzzling dedication to "W.H." at the start of the Sonnets, while Stephen thinks over the money he has just spent and admits (in thought only) his envy of Mulligan. Stephen's telegram to Mulligan, which expresses his resentment at

---

1. The following Latin words mean "Love genuinely wishes another's good, on account of which we desire these things." See Ellmann's Preface to the new edition, page xii.

money he has lent (and perhaps his guilt at clothes he has borrowed), is read aloud.[1] Mulligan imitates an old Irishwoman—the sort of character John Synge created—and Stephen thinks of Paris encounters with Synge.

Meanwhile Bloom has turned up in the Library, looking for his crossed-keys ad. Lyster goes out courteously to serve him while Mulligan exclaims "The sheeny!" (605). Back to Shakespeare. Stephen recreates for his listeners the richness of Elizabethan life, mentally setting the playwright's sexual conquests against his own encounters with Parisian prostitutes ("Cours la Reine...", 641). If Shakespeare did not resent Ann Hathaway's infidelity, Stephen asks, why the famous bequest to her of the second-best bed? Eglinton tries to explain, in a brief passage of blank verse. Stephen defends his idea by establishing Shakespeare's interest in property and property rights, including his rights over his wife. In her old age Ann Hathaway knew guilt and read pious books, Stephen continues; she felt the "agenbite of inwit" Stephen himself has felt. The thought of his mother's death forces itself into his consciousness, as it so often does. With an effort Stephen returns to Shakespeare, speculating more wildly than ever on paternity and confusing even himself ("What the hell are you driving at?", 846). He continues with a clearer exposition of Shakespeare's brothers' misdeeds. Their names, the names given to villains in the plays, are significant.

Father Dineen calls Lyster out once more; Stephen thinks of his own brother. Tiring, thirsty, he concludes his theorizing with a last statement of the essential Shakespearean theme, "banishment from the heart, banishment from home" (1000). Banishment, we may note, is the essential Odyssean theme, and the condition in which Stephen now suffers and glories; even Bloom knows he is banished from his home until after Molly's assignation. Stephen concludes his literary performance with a grand peroration about meeting strangers who always turn out to be, in some sense, ourselves. In his last phrase, "a wife unto himself," he leaves an opening to Mulligan, who starts to scribble a playlet about masturbation.

The question of whether Stephen will publish an article on his theory being left open, he and Mulligan exit. They overhear Lyster's talk with Father Dineen and Mulligan spits out his scorn of Eglinton, the Abbey

---

1. Ironically, the attack on debtorship in the telegram is itself adapted from and thus indebted to George Meredith's novel *The Ordeal of Richard Feverel.* Is Stephen aware of the irony? Or is the joke turned against him?

Theatre, monks. Should Stephen, recollecting something he left out ("Afterwit," 1137), go back? It is too late. Mulligan berates Stephen for not writing flatteringly of Lady Gregory (Mulligan's own hatreds and scorns are always expressed in private), and we get a reading of the masturbation playlet, *Everyman His Own Wife*. At the conclusion of the chapter, Stephen has reached the symbolic moment of parting from Mulligan, and to assist his decision a man—Bloom, now re-assuming the role of Ulysses—passes between them. It is the Wandering Jew, Mulligan warns, and furthermore he has erotic designs on Stephen, but Stephen thinks of his dream of creamfruit and a street of harlots. The dream will come true in *Circe*: Stephen will meet Bloom, the mourning son will find the dispossessed father.

[10] *Wandering Rocks* (pages 180–209)

In the *Odyssey* the witch Circe warns Ulysses of the Prowling Rocks, or Drifters, which crush ships and prevent even birds from flying by. Ulysses avoids them by taking the equally dangerous route between Scylla and Charybdis. (In a parallel myth, which Joyce may well have had in mind, the Symplegades or Clashing Rocks impede the Argonauts on their way to the Black Sea and the Golden Fleece.) *Wandering Rocks* examines civic flotsam. The drifting Dubliners here are too busy with their ordinary midafternoon activities to think much, except for Father Conmee at the start, Tom Kernan, Miss Dunne, Stephen, and Bloom in the middle, and Master Patrick Dignam at the end. The rest of the Dubliners act and speak, walk about, react to the city's sights—for example, the carriages of the English viceroy and his party issuing from Phoenix Park. The nineteen vignettes of the episode give a more comprehensive picture of Dublin than any we have yet been shown. In various locations about the city, but at roughly the same moment, Dubliners circulate ("blood" is the organ of the episode, as the *Ulysses* ground plan tells us). They do not so much impede Bloom as reveal themselves.

Joyce's narrative here employs abrupt interruptions, which sometimes give a strongly cinematic effect. In the midst of showing us one Dublin sight, he will shift without warning to another and apparently unrelated sight, just for a moment, as in the midst of one scene a film editor cuts without warning to another, to suggest what is happening elsewhere. For example, in the midst of a vignette about the typist Miss Dunne, five sandwichmen advertising Wisdom Hely's suddenly appear (377). With such shifts Joyce emphasizes the simultaneity of events and the interconnectedness of Dublin life. Sometimes he does more. We glimpse a one-legged sailor, hear him singing for alms, and then for the space of a single sentence are shown J. J. O'Molloy still trying to arrange his loan, this time from Ned Lambert (236). Thus Joyce juxtaposes two beggars. *Wandering Rocks* is full of discrepancy turning into likeness.

*   *   *

The first Dubliner displayed in the chapter is Father Conmee, seen taking his charitable but also complacent way to Artane on the city's outskirts. He wants to oblige Martin Cunningham by trying to enroll young Patrick Dignam in school. He encounters the one-legged sailor and others, thinks about the "Invincible ignorance" of Protestants (71), boards a tram, and recalls the romantic history of Jesuit houses, turning himself into the romantic figure of "Don John Conmee" in the process. Did the Countess of Belvedere betray her husband with his brother? Conmee's question revives the sexual issue Stephen elaborated in discussing *Hamlet* and anticipates cases of adultery yet to come in *Wandering Rocks*, in a book Bloom will buy, for instance. The priest remembers reading his office while he was rector at Clongowes School. His thoughts, as we have seen, take the sonorous, parallel form of psalmody (184). Back in the present, Conmee reads the office Nones, beginning with an Our Father and a Hail Mary, then proceeding to the twentieth and twenty-first sections of Psalm 119 (Psalm 118 in the Latin Vulgate Bible). Finally Conmee meets a flushed young couple, who have been courting under the hedge.

Corny Kelleher, who works for O'Neill the undertaker (and perhaps, as an informer, for the police), passes the time of day with Constable 57C. At the same moment Molly's plump arm throws a coin from a window at 7 Eccles Street.

The one-legged begging sailor makes his rounds, growling out the phrase "For England, home and beauty," which we will later hear repeated. Street urchins put Molly's coin in his cap.

Katey and Boody Dedalus, Stephen's sisters, enter the squalid Dedalus house, where their sister Maggy is doing a wash. Katey and Boody have had no success pawning Stephen's books with the queenly Mrs M'Guinness, but the family has been given some pea soup in charity, and they eat. Boody breaks chunks of bread, and we are granted a quick look at the crumpled throwaway which Bloom cast into the Liffey in *Lestrygonians* (8.57), just after he broke cakes for the hungry gulls. The throwaway has become a "skiff" on its way out to sea.

Blazes Boylan buys a fancy fruit-basket as a gift for Molly, and Joyce's phrasing—"bedded the wicker basket," "shamefaced peaches"—suggests the nature of their coming rendezvous. Boylan flirts roguishly with the shopgirl and leaves with a red flower between his teeth.

Stephen talks with the music teacher Almidano Artifoni, an older man who tells Stephen in Italian that, when young, he, too, had these ideas…he, too, was convinced that the world was a pigsty. It's too bad, he adds, because Stephen's voice would be a source of income. Instead, Stephen is sacrificing himself. A bloodless sacrifice, Stephen responds, but he agrees to think about what Artifoni has said—presumably, some words of advice about a musical career. The two men part affectionately, with Stephen giving spoken thanks and a thought tribute ("Human eyes," 356). Meanwhile bandsmen in Scottish garb are getting ready for a concert.

Miss Dunne, a typist working for Boylan, puts paper in her machine and thinks about the Wilkie Collins novel she is reading, then about the music-hall star on a poster. She gives a message to Boylan when he telephones.

In the ancient council chamber of St Mary's Abbey, now a warehouse, Ned Lambert is holding forth to the reverend Hugh C. Love, a clergyman with antiquarian interests who wishes to take some photographs of the site. J. J. O'Molloy enters, but before he can ask for his loan, Lambert starts to sneeze. Halfway through this episode (425), we glimpse the long face of John Howard Parnell, the great Parnell's brother, who will appear in a tea shop later in the chapter. Parnell gazes at a chessboard. Behold another relic of the past.

Tom Rochford is showing Nosey Flynn and M'Coy his newly invented device for indicating which "turn" (or act) is on at a music hall: numbered disks shoot down grooves and then wobble to a stop. Lenehan will sound out Boylan, apparently about this machine, in the Ormond Hotel. Lenehan and M'Coy discuss Rochford's act of heroism in rescuing a man from a gaspipe, then the Gold Cup race; the favorite is the "game filly" Sceptre. They spot Bloom looking at used books, and the conversation turns to Molly, another game filly, whose ample charms Lenehan was once able to sample as they drove back from a party. The anecdote is at Bloom's expense, of course—he was too busy explaining the stars to notice what Lenehan was doing with his wife—but Lenehan nevertheless finishes with a tribute to him. There is a touch of the artist about Bloom, he admits (582). Using the cliché, "a cultured allroundman," Lenehan innocently takes the reader back to ancient Greece and Homer's favorite epithet for Odysseus, *polytropos*, "of many turns."

The artist is at this moment seeking, from a hawker's cart, a new book for Molly. She has had *Fair Tyrants* by James Lovebirch. The title and authorial name appeal especially to Bloom; by Joycean coincidence, he has just been examining *Tales of the Ghetto*, by Leopold von Sacher Masoch, whose interest in these matters produced the term "masochism." We are given excerpts from a shocker Molly might like, *Sweets of Sin.* Bloom himself, liking it, is driven to heavy breathing and excited mental exclamations, including, pathetically, "Young! Young!" (625). He buys the book from the coughing and blear-eyed shopman. From this point onward, "Raoul" in *Sweets of Sin* will loom large in Bloom's mind as a type of exaggerated and exotic virility.

Dilly Dedalus, still another of Stephen's sisters, accosts her father near Dillon's auctionrooms, outside of which the servant or lacquey keeps ringing his handbell. Simon Dedalus offers a sardonic paternal interest in her posture, but Dilly will not be put off and gets a shilling out of him, then a bitter joke about finding money, then two more pennies, which she is supposed to spend on milk and a bun. Simon goes off mimicking the nuns who, he thinks, have turned his daughter against him.

Tom Kernan, the Protestant tea salesman, thinks of the business call he has just made and takes pleasure in the neat correctness of his dress. He has had a good drop of gin from his customer. Recalling "bad times" in Dublin, he imagines the dashing young aristocrats of former days, including the rebel Lord Edward Fitzgerald, who escaped from Major Sirr but was eventually betrayed by the "sham squire" Francis Higgins. We are granted one line from the patriotic ballad "The Croppy Boy," later to be performed in *Sirens.* As if to prove that aristocracy has not passed from the world, the viceregal cavalcade goes by. Joyce's wording wittily captures the riders' up-and-down motions: "outriders leaping, leaping in their, in their saddles" (795).

Stephen observes jewels in a cobwebby shop window and creates a sensual scene from the sight. As men dig gems from the earth, he wrests old images from their burial places. And he challenges God ("Bawd and butcher," 826) to shatter him. Suddenly he comes upon a bookcart and decides to look for the pawned volumes he was given as school prizes. But a book of magical lore detains him, with its strange talisman to gain a woman's love: "*Se el yilo...*" (849). Amidst the gibberish the words "*Amor me solo!* " stand out. Though ungrammatical, they seem to mean "Love me alone!" A real woman whom he ought to love, his sister Dilly, then greets him, and in one of the most accessible and moving passages in the whole novel, they speak. She, like Stephen, has an inquiring mind—"quick, far and daring" eyes—and she wishes to follow modestly in his path, learning French. Stephen tells himself to show no surprise at her ambition. Chardenal's French primer is all right, he gloomily allows. What he thinks is that her helplessness will drown him, drag him under into misery. What he feels is again remorse, the "agenbite of inwit." The word "We" stands all by itself on line 878, an emblem of family pain very different from the "We" Bloom cherishes in *Aeolus* (7.37), an emblem of momentary alliance.

Simon Dedalus encounters "Father" Bob Cowley, who owes money to the "gombeen man" or usurer Reuben J. Dodd ("With a broken back," 891). Cowley self-consciously strokes the moustache he would not be wearing were he still a real priest.[1] Up comes the bass baritone (or "bass barreltone") Ben Dollard, who is going to put in a good word with the subsheriff Long John Fanning and perhaps get Cowley more time to pay. After singing a deep note, Dollard reminds them that Cowley's landlord (the reverend Hugh C. Love, as it happens) has the first claim on Cowley; Reuben J. Dodd's writ for payment of debt is worth nothing.

Martin Cunningham is "cracking the whip," trying to get up his collection for the Dignam family. To this fund Bloom has pledged and paid the considerable sum of five shillings. We hear that the city council ("the conscript fathers") is debating the Irish language. Cunningham tries to get money out of Long John Fanning, but the latter cannot remember Dignam.

Buck Mulligan and Haines have tea. As they sit down they notice John Howard Parnell quietly playing chess. Why has Stephen's mind lost its balance, producing such a fantastic view of *Hamlet?* The priests drove him insane with their visions of hell, Mulligan answers. Stephen will never

---

1. Robert M. Adams, *Surface and Symbol: The Consistency of James Joyce's Ulysses* (New York: Oxford University Press, 1962), p. 52.

capture the true Greek balance, the "Attic note" (1073), Mulligan thinks, eating hungrily, but he will write something in ten years.

Cashel Boyle O'Connor Fitzmaurice Tisdall Farrell wends his crazy way through Dublin, always walking outside the lampposts. "*Coactus volui*," he mutters (1113), "I have willed it under constraint," Farrell being one of the novel's compulsives, one of its prisoners of routine. He bumps into a blind stripling and is roundly cursed.

The late Patrick Dignam's son, also named Patrick, brings porksteaks home and thinks about the dullness of mourning. He is distracted by the poster of a prizefight between the "puckers" (boxers) Myler Keogh and Sergeantmajor Bennett, of whom we will hear later, and then he spies Boylan. The collar of his unfamiliar mourning costume keeps springing up. At last his mind focuses on his father's death ("Poor pa," 1172).

Having begun with one of Stephen's masters, the Roman Catholic Church, the chapter closes with another, the Imperial British State. The viceregal cavalcade, of which various Dubliners have had glimpses during the episode, finally appears in full panoply. Lord and Lady Dudley and their party leave Phoenix Park to be saluted, politely or sardonically, by among others Kernan and Richie Goulding, the filthy Poddle River, Miss Kennedy and Miss Douce (barmaids in the Ormond Hotel, who will figure largely in the next episode), Simon Dedalus, the reverend Hugh C. Love (whose "obeisance" is rendered in suitably antiquarian terms), Gerty MacDowell (who will appear in *Nausicaa*), Tom Rochford, Dilly Dedalus, Boylan with the admiration of his eyes, Patrick Dignam, and Patrick Dignam's collar. Sounding in the background, from a band of unseen "brazen highland laddies," is "My Girl's a Yorkshire Girl," a tune we will hear, much transformed, in *Circe*.

[11] *Sirens* (pages 210–239)

As befits an episode about the lure of song, *Sirens* is full of quasi-musical devices, beginning with an "overture" on the first two pages, which summarizes all the themes to be developed later. Later in the chapter Joyce imitates repetition and variation, as in three sad sentences about Miss Kennedy twisting her hair (81), and *staccato*, as in "Will? You? I. Want. You. To" (1096). He blends words together more or less as notes are blended in chords ("joygush, tupthrob," 709) and insistently repeats language for its sound value alone ("Lenehan round the sandwichbell wound his round body round," 240). Forced or over-ingenious some of these equivalences may be, but there is nothing forced about the musical performances in the episode. With perfect naturalness Joyce's melodious characters gather together in the Ormond bar, lured by the barmaids Miss Douce and Miss Kennedy, the up-to-date counterparts of Homer's Sirens, past whom Ulysses had to sail, tied to the mast of his ship. Many a ship foundered on the original Sirens' rock; many a Dubliner loses himself in the pleasures of flirtation and song. The sentimental favorites performed here include "When first I saw that form endearing" from Flotow's opera *Marthe* and the patriotic ballad "The Croppy Boy." Throughout the episode the singers' notes join with (or clash against) all the miscellaneous sounds of a Dublin late afternoon, including the "steelyringing" hooves of the viceregal procession, the snapping of Miss Douce's garter, the "clapclipclap" of applause, the jingling of Blazes Boylan's carriage as it approaches the Ormond Hotel and then takes him off to his encounter with Molly, and the tapping of a blind man's cane along the pavement—the same blind stripling Bloom helped across the street. The tapping echoes through the last half of the chapter, unwelcome cue to the way Boylan is "tepping her tapping her topping her" (706).

*   *   *

"He's killed looking back," Miss Douce comments at the start of the episode (77), as she admires the tall fellow in the second carriage of the procession. It is the nature of Sirens to lure mariners to their deaths, and Miss Mina Kennedy (gold hair) and Miss Lydia Douce (bronze hair) wait behind what Joyce calls a "reef" of a counter, but they are victims as well as victimizers. It's the men "has the fine times," Miss Kennedy comments (84). For his insolence, they rebuke the bootboy bringing them their tea tray, and they discuss remedies for Miss Douce's sunburned skin. They giggle together at the memory of ridiculous men. Meanwhile Bloom approaches along the streets, thinking of his earlier glimpse of Stephen and Mulligan. Temporarily, he becomes "Greaseabloom," in token of the barmaids' laughing at greasy old fogies. Names constantly change form or are "transposed" in this episode, as in "Kennygiggles," "Big Benben," "Lidlydiawell." Joyce's focus is also constantly shifted. First we view the bar: Simon Dedalus enters, then Lenehan, who teases Miss Kennedy and ingratiatingly passes on news of Stephen. Then we are out in the streets: Bloom buys stationery to write to Martha and catches a glimpse of Boylan. Back inside the bar again, Simon wanders to the piano, newly tuned by a blind youth, and we hear snatches from his song: *"The bright stars fade... the morn is breaking"* (320). Like *Wandering Rocks*, *Sirens* cuts from Dubliner to Dubliner, sound to sound, with cinematic abruptness.

Boylan enters and simultaneously Bloom decides to join Richie Goulding at dinner in the Ormond restaurant. There he will enjoy the "best value in Dublin" while he sees without being seen. Much flirting follows at the bar, as Lenehan and Boylan admire Miss Douce's satin bust. After coy resistance she is talked into snapping her garter for them (*"Sonnez la cloche!,"* "sound the bell," 404). Boylan is off, with a jingle, leaving Miss Douce pensive and Bloom apprehensive ("Course nerves a bit," 446). Ben Dollard and Bob Cowley enter. Bloom turned in handy, Simon Dedalus comments to the group, when Dollard needed a pair of dress trousers and got them from the Blooms, then running a secondhand clothes business. (In a demonstration of narrative parallax, Joyce furnishes Bloom's version of this transaction on the next page.) Simon and the others talk of Molly; Bloom and Goulding eat; Ben Dollard sings "When love absorbs my ardent soul"; Miss Kennedy serves two gentlemen with stout. George Lidwell enters. Father Bob Cowley continues at the piano, drawing some miscellaneous musical reminiscences from Bloom. Goulding's whistling of the air "All is lost now" from *La Sonnambula* makes Bloom melancholy ("Yes: all is lost," 641), then sympathetic. In an episode full of characters regretting what they have lost, Bloom alone thinks of someone else's troubles.

Finally, after prompting (he is as coy a performer as Miss Douce), Simon Dedalus begins to sing "When first I saw that form endearing," the air which means much to Bloom in his current state. It is one version of love's old sweet song; it recalls his own Martha and his own "idle dreaming"; it disturbs him and yet offers him, like the statues in the Museum and the curved wood in Davy Byrne's pub, the serene refuge of art ("good to hear," 677). Tenors get women "by the score," Bloom thinks, consciously or unconsciously punning. He himself first saw Molly's form endearing in a game of musical chairs. Dedalus' long-held *"Come...!"* soars high, bringing together performer Simon and listener Leopold in a single ecstatic "Siopold!" A few lines later Simon will become "Lionel Simon," after the character who sings the air in the opera. Richie Goulding praises his brother-in-law's voice while Bloom fiddles with a rubber band, finally snapping it. Miss Douce, ambivalent like so many characters in *Ulysses*, feels "reproachful, pleased" at Lidwell's attentions (813).

Could Bloom explain music to Martha in mathematical terms? The bald hard-of-hearing waiter Pat brings him pad, pen, and ink and, pretending to answer an ad in the *Freeman*, Bloom issues a siren call to his penpal sweetheart. He remembers to use the Greek ees he employed in his first missive to Martha: a tiny and appealing link back to Homer's Ulysses. In the next few paragraphs, "Bloom mur" precedes phrases he is murmuring aloud and pretending to write, "Henry wrote" what he is actually putting down. Is Martha naughty too?, Bloom asks. How will she punish him? He offers her the little gift of a postal order and ends with a plaintive postscript about being lonely. Meanwhile Miss Douce and Lidwell listen to a seashell's roar. Bloom considers the "chamber music" of Molly's waters tinkling into a chamber pot. As he wonders if Boylan has arrived ("Now. Maybe now," 984), a proud masculine knocking breaks rudely into the musical reverie, at least in Bloom's imagination. Literally, he hears the dark chords of Ben Dollard's rendition of "The Croppy Boy." In this ballad a Catholic youth confesses his "sins," including putting his country above his king, only to find that the priest is a yeoman captain in disguise; the youth is hanged. For two or three pages phrases from the ballad intermingle with Bloom's thoughts about the singer (a drunk but "no eunuch yet"), women and mirrors, Molly dressed in a low-cut gown for the opera, and his own sonless state. Like the croppy boy, Bloom is the last of his race. In an important brief passage Bloom is tempted by hope ("Too late now. Or if not?"), then realistic ("Soon I am old," 1069). Big abstract words like "hate" and "love" count for nothing next to the name of his lost one, Rudy.

The ballad gives the captain's reply to the croppy boy, accompanied by more stray thoughts on women and Bloom's observation of Miss Douce, who in all innocence fondles the smooth phallic beerpull. She thus provokes more sound of masculine crowing and more tapping. Could Miss Douce be Martha? No, Bloom concludes, and exits, glad to avoid the chorus of applause and the drinking after Ben has made his last appeal for tears and prayers. Now that the music is over (except for the "pwee" of the gas beginning to trouble him), Bloom has recovered his cautiousness. It is better to "give way only half way," he decides (1191). Like Ulysses, he will not lose control of himself and be wrecked on rocks. Back in the Ormond bar, they are once again discussing Molly.

On his way to buy a postal order for Martha, Bloom encounters a frowsy whore, then avoids her by turning to a shop window, where he sees printed the famous last words of the Irish patriot Robert Emmet: "When my country takes her place among the nations of the world, then and not till then let my epitaph be written. I have done" (1284). The cautious Bloom waits for the right moment ("then and not till then"), when a noisy tram passes, and emits a noisy "Pprrpffrrppffff"—which, whether it derives from burgundy or cider, expresses Joyce's opinion of gassy sentimentality.

[12] *Cyclops* (pages 240–283)

Much of this episode is rendered in the pungent street language of an anonymous Dublin drinker, a cynic with scarcely a good word for anyone. He and his cronies attack Bloom viciously, but in doing so only convince the reader of the latter's modest virtues. The five shillings he has donated to the Dignams might be forgotten were it not for Lenehan's slanderous remark that Bloom is off "Defrauding widows and orphans" (1622). Thus language in *Cyclops* turns against its users, a yet more obvious example being a threat to "crucify" Bloom for allegedly blaspheming Christ (1812).

Even stranger things happen to language in the chapter. Intermittently, Joyce interrupts the narrator with bravura linguistic performances of his own—broad parodies of an epic style, or of overblown newspaper writing, or of legal language, or of coy literary gossip, or of old-fashioned prizefight reporting. He stylizes prose to the point of absurdity, then beyond, since his interruptions sometimes grow ludicrously inconsistent, vulgar, or clumsy. Theosophic lore becomes business-like; high epic tones tumble. A parodied account of a hanging is fantastically flowery until the very end, when a character drops into the crudest Cockney: "God blimey if she aint a clinker …" (676). In particular Joyce devotes himself to gigantic lists. These represent a familiar convention of epic, the catalogue of names, but they tend to become anachronistic or facetious, so that a list of ancient Irish heroes and heroines beginning, properly enough, with Cuchulain, goes on to include Gautama Buddha and The Man that Broke the Bank at Monte Carlo (185).

All this linguistic playfulness seems in keeping with the natural style of the characters themselves. They say more than they need to, taking enormous pleasure in invective, hyperbole, and slang ("'Twas the prudent member gave me the wheeze," 211). The chapter's Polyphemus, a blowhard nicknamed "the Citizen," a fierce patriot and enthusiast for Gaelic sports, loves to get his tongue round highsounding phrases like "wine of the country" and "the memory of the dead"; he is always doing "the rapparee and Rory of the hill" (134), sounding off like a fiery Irish rebel of the eighteenth century, as the unimpressed narrator judges. Still, Joyce's parodies go beyond anything to be heard in Dublin, past or present. Like the headlines in *Aeolus*, they stand apart from events and characters and are meant to be taken on their own terms. What they abundantly demonstrate is Joycean virtuosity with comic language.

In narrating a contest between brute force and inventive courage, the chapter follows Homer closely. Ulysses and his men were trapped in the cave of Polyphemus the Cyclops, a giant with one eye. Most of the Greeks escaped by hiding under the bellies of sheep, after Ulysses guilefully made the giant drunk and put his eye out with a sharpened burnt stick (represented in modern-day Dublin by Bloom's cigar). Foolishly, however, Ulysses taunted the Cyclops, who hurled a boulder after the Greeks and nearly capsized their boat. Bloom will make a similar escape, a similar taunt.

*   *   *

It is five o'clock. The narrator and Joe Hynes share a laugh at a "little jewy" trying to recover a debt from an old plumber. After Joyce provides a mock legal contract, growing (as most of the parodies grow) out of the subject being discussed, and after a mock epic celebration of Irish riches, the two characters proceed to Barney Kiernan's pub, there to meet the Citizen and his mangy dog, Garryowen. The Citizen is presented as a giant hero of Irish myth, though in reality he is a tolerated eccentric, "one-eyed" in the extremity of his views,[1] waiting for someone to buy him a drink. For a wonder, Hynes has money: following Bloom's "tip," he's won a packet betting on Throwaway. The Citizen issues the first of several denunciations of England and of Irish institutions (like *The Irish Independent*) that toady to the English. Alf Bergan appears with news about Breen, still incensed at the insulting postcard someone sent him. The barman Terry serves him a Guinness ("a crystal cup full of the foamy ebon ale" in the epic version,

---

1. As Harry Blamires notes in *The New Bloomsday Book* (London: Routledge, 1996), "one-eyedness" runs through the chapter, and not least through Joyce's parodies, each "a single fashion of utterance pushed to its extremest limits" (p. 113).

281), and Bergan produces letters from public executioners offering their services to the high sheriff of Dublin. Bergan has just seen Paddy Dignam, though the rest know Paddy was buried this very morning. The hint of ghostliness stimulates Joyce's long parody of a séance. Amid theosophist jargon, spirits are summoned and reveal a "heavenworld" with ludicrous modern conveniences, all spelled out in mock Sanskrit.

The drinkers have spotted Bloom outside, walking up and down and waiting to meet Martin Cunningham in order to arrange a detail of Paddy Dignam's insurance. Once inside, the "prudent member," so called because of his Masonic connections, demonstrates his prudence by refusing a drink, though he does accept a cigar. Back to discussion of hangmen and their victims. "By science" Bloom explains the erect penises of hanged men, and the Citizen seizes the chance for more political gassing. The two men start arguing, but before we hear anything the narrator treats us to a nasty anecdote about Bloom (a failed attempt to gain an old woman's money and to teach a young man the evils of drink), and then Joyce treats us to a hugely funny account of a public hanging. Event by fantastic event, journalistic cliché by journalistic cliché, he goes through all possible melodramatic turns of plot and all possible national names (the Chinese delegate Hi Hung Chang, the American Hiram Y. Bomboost, and so on). Back in reality at Kiernan's, the Citizen celebrates the Irish language, and Bloom is blamed for refusing to treat his friends. Garryowen growls; the growls turn into verses praised in yet another parody. There are more drinks, and the narrator thinks of new reasons to despise Bloom, such as his attempt to sell lottery tickets or his knowingness, his tendency to tell everyone how to do everything. But the narrator also despises Bob Doran, the trapped husband of the *Dubliners* story "A Boarding House," who has been coming out of an alcoholic stupor throughout the episode and whose miseries are now briefly related.

Bloom wants to see Councillor Nannetti, to complete arrangements for the Keyes ad, but the latter is on his way to the English Parliament in London, a bit of news leading to a parodied parliamentary interchange. The drinkers praise the Citizen's shot-putting, leading to a fulsomely reported debate on the revival of ancient sports. Then comes discussion of the Keogh-Bennett boxing match, leading to a nineteenth-century account of fisticuffs, with wonderful periphrases like "tapped some lively claret." Amid talk of Boylan, Hynes asks about the concert tour, and Bloom is forced to admit Boylan is "an excellent man to organise" (995).

J. J. O'Molloy and Ned Lambert enter to more discussion of Breen and his postcard. O'Molloy thinks a suit for libel might be successful; the Citizen pities not just Mrs Breen but any woman marrying a "pishogue" (1058). The word means merely a "fairy" or "someone bewitched," but the Citizen apparently intends a sharper insult as he glares at Bloom—someone non compos mentis? An unmanly man? Trouble is coming between them, the narrator sees. After an interlude for discussion of a courtcase, in realistic and epic style, the Citizen comes out with his anti-semitism: "We want no more strangers in our house" (1150). Bloom keeps quiet. Is he stung particularly by the attacks on "a dishonoured wife" as the cause of all Irish misfortunes? Meanwhile Bergan and Terry are ogling the dishonored Mrs Norman W. Tupper in a *Police Gazette*.

John Wyse Nolan and Lenehan enter in time to hear an attack on English "syphilisation." Lenehan has lost money on Sceptre in the Gold Cup. Bloom begins a warning against hypocrisy but is overwhelmed by the Citizen's rapturous celebration of old Irish industries, in a speech nearly as extravagant in style as Joyce's parodies. Forests are mentioned, and Joyce contributes an extravagant account of Miss Fir Conifer's wedding. The punishments used in the English navy come in for savage criticism, and Joyce contributes a blasphemous creed ("They believe in rod, the scourger almighty...", 1354). Now the dispute between the Citizen and Bloom grows warmer. The former calls excitedly for the use of force against force, and for Irish Americans to join the fight against the "whitelivered Saxons," the French ("never worth a roasted fart") having proved such treacherous friends to Ireland. Bloom, ever a man of peace (even now he is still talking only to Nolan), decries persecution, hatred of nations, but is rudely asked what his own nation is. "Ireland," he answers, and the Citizen spits. He takes out a handkerchief (elaborately described), and Bloom begins to stand up for his persecuted race. But he will not condone force, the very opposite of "that that is really life" (1483). By this phrase Bloom means Stephen's word known to all men, love. As if embarrassed by such a strong avowal he steps out to look for Cunningham.

Scorn for "universal love" follows his exit, then scorn for sanctimonious preachers, then the reading of a lampoon version of an African chief's visit to England. Lenehan announces that Bloom, the "dark horse," has gone to get his winnings on Throwaway. They are perfectly capable of despising him simultaneously as a bettor in the know and as a "whiteeyed kaffir," not man enough to bet at all. The narrator leaves to "pumpship" and while in the back of the pub yard also relieves himself of more scorn of Bloom. A brief interruption for Martin Cunningham's late arrival (he and friends are greeted by "mine host" in medieval style), and then the slanders intensify. Cunningham calls Bloom "perverted" while the Citizen wonders who fathered his children. However false the picture of a Jew not knowing "if he's a father or a mother" (1648), Bloom does embody feminine (and especially maternal) traits, as later passages of the novel will testify.

After the cue "God bless all here" (1673) a long catalogue of priests, saints, miracles, and saintly emblems delays the finale of the argument. Hidden away in the verbiage are such oddities as "S. Marion Calpensis" (Molly, born in Gibraltar or Calpe) and, beginning with "S. Martin of Tours" (1694), a saintly catalogue of all the customers in the pub, not forgetting "S. Owen Caniculus" or Saint Owen the little dog—the mangy beast Garryowen.

At last the finale comes when the Citizen insults Bloom directly, with "Don't tell anyone [about your secret winnings]," 1762). Cunningham tries to hustle Bloom out. In the street, mounted in their carriage, they receive more shouted insults, and Bloom is for once rattled enough to shout back a list of distinguished Jews, including Christ and his Father, or his "uncle," as he corrects himself immediately. "Christ was a jew like me" (1808) he announces, with uncharacteristic, imprudent, but Ulysses-like defiance.[1] The Citizen hurls imprecations, then a biscuitbox, Joyce rendering the action as epically as possible, with an earthquake to mark the catastrophe. At the end Bloom makes his escape, ascending "to the Glory" like Elijah and surrounded by Scriptural phraseology. He is amid angels but also (for all of his linguistic extravagance, Joyce rarely stops being a realist) in Little Green Street, and he is safe.

[13] *Nausicaa* (pages 284–313)

In Homer's epic, Ulysses, the survivor of storms and shipwrecks, is washed up naked on the island of the Phaeacians. The beautiful princess Nausicaa is playing ball on the beach with her maidens. Ulysses advances to

---

1. Earlier, when Bloom commented on people who "can see the mote in others' eyes but they can't see the beam in their own" (1237), he aligns himself both with Ulysses (who put the beam in Polyphemus' eye) and with Christ (see Luke 6:42).

speak with her but not before he covers himself in gentlemanly fashion with a branch. Receiving him with great interest (Athena has previously sent her a romantic dream), Nausicaa leads him to her father's palace. In Joyce's epic, Bloom is equally a survivor and a gentleman. He has weathered the sight of Boylan going off to Molly in *Sirens* and the Citizen's taunts in *Cyclops* and has done his duty by the Dignam family, visiting their house to make insurance arrangements. Now he loiters on nearby Sandymount strand, meditating, unconsciously displaying his gentlemanly looks and attractive melancholy for Gerty MacDowell.

Though no princess, Gerty reads the *Princess Novelette*, following its suggestions about cosmetics and half believing its love stories ("patrician suitors at her feet vying with one another to pay their devoirs to her," 103). In the first half of the episode Joyce describes Gerty and her thoughts in the subromantic style of the magazines she reads, a style "almost maddening in its sweetness" (511), as Joyce comments about her dainty head of nutbrown tresses. No cliché is omitted, no chance for sentimentality missed. As she thinks about her life at home or the dark gentleman on the beach, Gerty tries hard to stay genteel, but sometimes she loses her temper, reveals her commonness ("The colours were done something lovely," 337), or makes a Martha-like mistake ("the perfume of those incense," 410). At these moments the tone drops bathetically. *Nausicaa*, like *Cyclops*, offers an elevated style that cannot quite stay elevated. One of its subjects is the failure of human beings to live up to the language they choose for themselves.

*   *   *

The sun is setting as Gerty and her friends Edy Boardman and Cissy Caffrey look after their young brothers and enjoy a "cosy chat" on "matters feminine." Tommy and Jacky Caffrey fight over a sandcastle. Edy comforts Tommy when he cries and helps him urinate behind the pushcar where "the gentleman," Bloom, can't see. (In this episode, disagreeable realities invariably impose themselves on romantic poses.) Edy says that Gerty is Tommy's sweetheart—an arch hint that Gerty is not Reggy Wylie's sweetheart. That young man's father is keeping him in to study, and so he no longer rides his freewheel up and down in front of Gerty's window. Thoughts of this love that might have been put Gerty in a wistful mood, though judging by her daydream about wedding bells (196) she has not entirely given up hope. Too ladylike to speak back to Edy, she takes comfort in imagining a husband more manly and mature than Reggy, a man with hair slightly flecked with gray. For such a man she yearns. For such a man she would cook her "griddlecakes done to a goldenbrown hue" (224). On and on her daydream goes, in a series of breathless clauses connected by "ands."

Meanwhile a men's temperance retreat is going on in a nearby church. Its litanies and prayers will be overheard throughout the rest of the episode, in a counterpoint matching religious with romantic sentimentality, the Virgin behind the altar with the virgin on the beach—a virgin whom Bloom will, in his own way, adore. (Mary's color is blue, and Gerty is wearing an electric blue blouse, thanks to the advice of the *Lady's Pictorial*.) At the sound of voices and organ, Gerty thinks sadly of her father, a victim of drink, then like Eveline in the *Dubliners* story she recalls happier family moments. At home she is a good daughter, helping her mother, doing chores, tacking up a picture of a lady and a gentleman in the privy, or "that place." She goes there "for a certain purpose" but thinks of "oldtime chivalry" (336). In similar circumstances Bloom read "Matcham's Masterstroke."

Speaking of Bloom, that "gentleman in black" now tries to throw the twins' ball back to Cissy but only gets it as far as Gerty. Is this a case of "accidentally on purpose" (485), to use Gerty's later phrase? Bloom's face seems the saddest she has ever seen. Her reverie is disrupted when "his infant majesty" requires "toilet formalities"; Gerty cannot maintain this highfalutin' tone and wishes only that they would "take their squalling baby home out of that" (404). But Bloom still gazes on her with his dark eyes, and she thinks him a foreigner, a mourner, a sinner. She could help him forget the past. Gerty remembers confessing her own sins to another attractive older man, Father Conroy. Cissy chases after the twins, tossing her hair behind but failing to draw the dark stranger's gaze from Gerty, who blushes. Is it time for the girls to go? "Madcap" Cissy goes boldly over to Bloom, but his watch has stopped at 4:30, the time of Molly's and Boylan's tryst ("Was that just when he, she?", 848).

As they prepare to leave, Edy asks Gerty if she is heartbroken about Reggy and gets a pert answer back. Gerty could easily chuck him aside. But the twilight and the chiming bells soften her mood, and she thinks of her girlish treasure trove, dreams no one knows of, poetry. Fireworks go off. Gerty remains on her rock, tingling at Bloom's passionate glance and leaning far back to entice him: only he is there to see her "graceful beautifully shaped legs" (698). There is nothing sinful about her excitement—it is on account of "that other thing coming on" (713), her menstrual period—so she bends back further and further, trembles, longs to cry out her love. When Bloom reaches his own sexual climax, a Roman candle bursts in rapture in the sky.

In a particularly dramatic demonstration of parallax, Joyce now gives us Bloom's thoughts of Gerty, beginning with the observation that she moves slowly because she is lame, "that one shortcoming" in her appearance Gerty could not quite be open about, even in thought (650). "Poor girl!" he thinks sympathetically. From the poor girl, the accomplice of his masturbatory love, Bloom proceeds to ruminations on women in general. He considers their odd cravings, their sexual excitement, their dressing up, their cattiness to each other, and especially their menstruation ("That's the moon," 782). Recomposing his wet shirt, he wonders if he should have spoken with Gerty but then remembers past encounters and seems to conclude that it's better to love from a distance. Women never sit on benches marked Wet Paint, Bloom thinks (prudent himself, he notices prudence in others), and they love to look in mirrors. The three-year-old Milly Bloom stood before the mirror and said "*Me have a nice pace*" (927).

In much of what he thinks, of course, Bloom sharply differentiates himself from Gerty. He achieves an objectivity she lacks ("See ourselves as others see us," 1058) and joins aspects of life she would keep separate, as when, bringing religion down from the altar, he observes that prayers and ads are alike effective because repeated. He is knowing, she appallingly naive; he down-to-earth, she coyly euphemistic. He has been married to Molly and fathered children while she has read Miss Cummins' *The Lamplighter*.[1] Yet Joyce does not keep Bloom and Gerty entirely separate. They both make the sardonic comment "*Tableau!* "(486, 815), as if to say "What a picture!" And in a different mood they both acknowledge that beauty is transient, youth fleeting. Touched by poetry, Gerty feels the years "slipping by for her, one by one" (649). Touched by Gerty, Bloom knows that love lasts "only a few years till they settle down to potwalloping and papa's pants will soon fit Willy" (952).

---

1. Joyce mentions this particular romance because it supplied him with the name "Gerty" and perhaps hints about a girlish style. See Gifford and Seidman, p. 384.

In his pages of interior monologue Bloom wanders somewhat haphazardly from topic to topic. Could Gerty be his penpal Martha? Is Nurse Callan still at the hospital? Is there a magnetic influence between people? (In the image of a compass needle attracted by a steel fork he finds first an emblem of man and woman, then a memory of Molly and Blazes.) What is the perfume Gerty has wafted across the air to him? What smell do men give off? He ponders bats and thinks he would like to be the rock Gerty sat on. He remembers an excursion trip on the *Erin's King* with Milly and a game of charades at Dolphin's Barn with the youthful Molly. Bloom acted out "Rip Van Winkle" (1112), Rip being a hero who returned home after an absence of twenty years, like Ulysses. More often than anyone else, Molly comes to his mind, Molly at fifteen, kissing lieutenant Mulvey in Gibraltar, or explaining why she married Bloom ("Because you were so foreign from the others," 1209). Howth Head, place of their first lovemaking, looms on the horizon. In memories our hero does what he can to counter the bittersweet transience of life.

Bloom wanders mentally because he is tired and let down after his sexual excitement. For once he is not moving briskly through Dublin, seeing things which start new trains of thought, but rather keeping still, savoring the evening. He draws on recollection and imagination, like Stephen, who nine hours earlier, in *Proteus*, walked on this same beach. Both men examine seawrack, tide pools, "rocks with lines and scars and letters" (1261). By coincidence of setting Joyce draws his two characters together, and by coincidence of thought: Bloom's "History repeats itself" (1093) echoes the lesson of *Nestor*, and his "Think you're escaping and run into yourself" (1110) repeats Stephen's claim at the end of *Scylla and Charybdis*, that "We walk through ourselves..." (9.1044). Even Bloom's tribute to Gerty's stockings, "O, those transparent!" (1261), hints at Stephen's more abstruse speculations about the diaphane and adiaphane.

Finding an old stick, Bloom turns it into a stylus and begins a message to Gerty, who might return to read it. Then, changing his mind, he attempts self-definition, writing "I....AM. A" on the sand (1264). "I am a married man"? "I am a Jew"? "I am a cuckold"? "I am a stick in the mud"? All are possibilities, along with the more obvious "I am a naughty boy," which would follow directly from the recollections of Martha's letter in the previous line, or "I am a fool," which he has admitted at line 1098. But before finishing the sentence he stops and effaces the letters with his boot. Sand is a hopeless thing, and it is hopeless to think of meeting Gerty again.

"But it was lovely" (1272). There is time for a short snooze before he must leave for the maternity hospital. Bloom dreams, savoring all the sweet stickiness of his encounter with Gerty, confusing her with Molly. The temperance retreat is over, and on the mantelpiece of the priest's house a cuckoo clock sounds nine, an insistent reminder that, for all his wickedness with Gerty ("we two naughty," 1280), Bloom is still a cuckold.

[14] *Oxen of the Sun* (pages 314–349)

"Let us go south to Holles Street," the chapter begins, but it does so in a mixture of Latin and Celtic, because part of its purpose is to chart the development of prose. From the ancient languages and a cumbersome Latinate style ("Universally that person's acumen") on the first page, we progress to the alliterative manner of Old English ("Before born babe bliss had") on the second. Thereafter, stage by stage, style by style, Joyce replicates the history of his medium, ending, finally, with half-Irish, half-American slang. *Oxen of the Sun*, in other words, is built of linguistic parallaxes. It is elaborately and pedantically learned and gave the friends to whom Joyce first showed it immediate difficulties, as it gives difficulties to readers today. The important fact to hold on to is that, through all the shifts from one author's style to another's, Joyce's characters remain the same. Mulligan cavorts, Lenehan sponges. Stephen refers to a mother as "a dam to bear beastly" (250), repeating, even amid medieval trappings, that word of Mulligan's which has so wounded him. When we read of Bloom, "Loth to irk in Horne's hall hat holding the seeker stood" (86), we recognize our hero. As usual, he is deferential and unwilling to trouble. Joyce has simply rendered him in antique terms, as though he were a figure from an Old English poem. Later Bloom will metamorphose into a Bunyanesque Mr Cautious Calmer, then into an "alien" reviled in eighteenth-century pamphlet style, then into a participant in a nineteenth-century scientific debate. But he remains Bloom, even at the very end, when among the hard drinkers at Burke's pub, he takes a ginger cordial.

*   *   *

A language developing or "gestating" befits an episode about birth. The first paragraphs introduce the general theme of the "procreating function" and the measures civilized nations take to encourage easy births. Ireland has provided the Maternity Hospital in Holles Street, called "Horne's hall" because one of its directors is Andrew Horne. There Mina Purefoy has come to deliver "wombfruit"; there Bloom comes, led by sympathy and curiosity. While lightning from a summer thunderstorm flashes ("levin leaping," 81), he meets Nurse Callan, a figure from his past. He asks after Doctor O'Hare and learns of his death, leading to a warning about "that last end" in a parody of the medieval play *Everyman*. Mina Purefoy has been in labor three days, Nurse Callan informs him. Bloom wonders at the nurse's nine-years-prolonged virginity.

In an adjacent room, wonderingly described in the Middle English style of Sir John Mandeville, roisterers have gathered to talk and drink. They include young Doctor Dixon, who once treated Bloom for a bee-sting ("sore wounded in his breast by a spear," 129), Lenehan, Stephen, the medical students Madden and Lynch, Crotthers, and Punch Costello. A tin of sardines ("strange fishes withouten heads," 150) lies open on the table. Bloom is "Sir Leopold"—an antique title, of course, to match the rest of the passage, but also a tribute to his genuinely chivalric qualities. Possibly we should consider "Sir Leopold" Joyce's version of "As Barbara Cartland would put it, I love you madly," that is, his means of complimenting his hero in an age of lost innocence. Sir Leopold accepts beer but pours most of it in another's glass. He listens to their questionings or "aresouns." If mother and unborn child are both in danger of dying, which life has precedence? The child's, church dogma would answer, but the roisterers disagree. Bloom, asked for his opinion, cautiously evades a direct answer. And what about contraception, Stephen asks, all those "Godpossibled souls that we nightly impossibilise" (225)? Contraception is an act of impiety, an offense against God's commandment to be fruitful and multiply. It is therefore a link back to the *Odyssey*: in Homer's epic Ulysses' crewmen impiously kill the oxen sacred to the sun-god Helios and are punished with death. (Phrases in the episode like "bright one, light one" and "sunbright wellbuilt fair home" drive home the connection to Helios.)

Bawdy jokes greet Stephen's comments on contraception, but he does not laugh. "Orgulous" (proud) of his "mother Church," even though it has cast him out, he continues with a catalogue of classical and Catholic notions about engendering. Neither does Bloom laugh. He looks in sorrow at Stephen, now riotously wasting his life, and remembers his lost son Rudy. Linguistically, with "About that present time..." (277) we have reached the

Renaissance, and in a more modern-sounding and flexible prose Stephen now boasts of money he has earned from the sale of a song (his pay for teaching, actually). He praises the Blessed Virgin, the second Eve who won us, as opposed to the first Eve who sold us, then lapses into French blasphemy and a playing with words. Like a rude mechanical in an Elizabethan play, Punch Costello begins a bawdy catch, only to be reprimanded by Nurse Quigley and the whole company.

Why has Stephen, who after all shows the "mien of a frere" (192), not taken friar's orders? The young man drunkenly (and falsely, of course) boasts of his virginity, which provokes much chaffing from his companions and the quoting of a mock Latin anthem *Ut novetur sexus*..., "That the whole mystery of physical spirituality may become known" (347). Stephen continues to rhapsodize, sometimes blasphemously in Mulligan's style ("Greater love...no man hath that a man lay down his wife for his friend," 360). At other moments he sounds like the Authorized Version of the Bible or the elaborately learned Sir Thomas Browne ("Assuefaction minorates atrocities," 383). By mentioning a stranger who has sinned against the light, the Biblical pastiche hints obliquely at Bloom. All in all, it is a vintage Stephen performance, or an *Étienne chanson*, a "Stephen song" as Costello comments (401), a monologue full of highsounding language and whimsical parodies, clever, sacrilegious, touched by self-pity ("thou hast left me alone for ever," 379).

Thunder sounds, and in response to its elemental power Joyce's language becomes alliterative once again, briefly. Style matches events, in other words, a principle all of *Oxen of the Sun* obeys, though usually in more subtle fashion. Hearing the thunder, hiding his real fear, Stephen cries out against Blake's tyrannical God of the Old Testament, "old Nobodaddy." Calmer Bloom fails to soothe Young Boasthard Stephen, as Joyce now parodies Bunyan's *Pilgrim's Progress*, the great seventeenth-century masterpiece of religious allegory. Scientific as usual, Bloom attempts to explain away the thunder as a natural phenomenon. Meanwhile the company decides it does not fear the whore Bird-in-the-Hand because Preservative has given them "a stout shield of oxengut" (465), i.e., condoms.

All welcome the rain now falling, in the style of the chatty diarist Samuel Pepys. Bloom has dreamt of Molly wearing Turkish costume. We hear of Lenehan's habits, including his hunger. Searching for Deasy's letter in the newspaper, he manages to turn the conversation to cattle and hoof-

and-mouth disease, whereupon Bloom, Ulysses-like, protests against the slaughter of the beasts (567). For his part, Stephen travesties the letter he has sponsored as bullockbefriending bard, and subsequently Dixon and Lynch improvise a piece of foolery or an "Irish bull," a satiric parable of England's conquest of Ireland. Irish bulls are not meant to be completely intelligible—that is part of the joke—but we can summarize the main points of this one as follows: in the year 1155 the Pope Adrian IV, the Englishman Nicholas Breakspear, issued a papal bull granting overlordship of Ireland to the English King Henry II ("the lord Harry," 592). Harry the bull insists among other things that only green grass may grow in Ireland (a reference to English laws regulating Irish land use). Henry VIII appears in the story too, as a later Lord Harry who bosses the show and completes the conquest of Ireland. Stephen adds that since the women of the island were enthralled by the bull, their men had to emigrate to America.

Enter Mulligan and Alec Bannon, described in the eighteenth-century prose of the *Tatler* or *Spectator*. Extravagantly fooling as usual, Mulligan advertises his services as "fertiliser" to all the childless women of Ireland. Bannon sighs sentimentally (Joyce is parodying Laurence Sterne) for a girl with a "new coquette cap" (758)—Milly Bloom in Mullingar, who has received a new tam as a birthday present.[1] Young Dixon leaves, to attend the now-imminent delivery. Costello speaks vulgarly, but no sooner does Bloom express his disapproval of such insensitivity and his happiness at the impending birth, than he is savagely criticized. He becomes the target of an eighteenth-century pamphlet attack. What right has he, an alien, a cuckold, to make moral judgments? Joyce fails to indicate which of the characters present (if any) is responsible for the criticism, perhaps because the pamphlets he is imitating were so often anonymous or because the judgment originates in Bloom himself.

The birth is announced, in an imitation of the solemn periodic sentences of the historian Edward Gibbon, and afterwards comes a general discussion of births, obstetric accidents, congenital defects, and Siamese twins. Then suddenly, with the mention of Haines and his dream of a black panther, the style turns Gothic. Joyce is first ludicrously portentous and mystifying, then slips into stage Irish, and finally concludes with a flatly prosaic explanation ("The mystery was unveiled," 1032). After these

---

1. *Marchand de capotes* (776) means "cloak merchant," but as Gifford and Seidman point out (p. 427) *capotes* is also slang for "condoms," so the conversation is less about rainwear than about the chapter's main theme, contraception.

excitements we have the nostalgic tone of the nineteenth-century essayist Charles Lamb, a tone apt for Bloom's memories of his youth. But the memories turn darker when Bloom recalls the prostitute Bridie Kelly, his first "love." In this stretch the stylistic imitations come thick and fast: Gothicism and Lamb, then De Quincey's dreamy style ("The voices blend and fuse," 1078) and Walter Savage Landor's employment of Greek names. Topics, too, shift rapidly. Stephen categorizes himself as bullockbefriending bard; Lenehan mourns Sceptre's failure in the Gold Cup; Vincent Lynch rhapsodizes about a rural tryst with his love. He and she, it turns out, were the couple Father Conmee encountered in *Wandering Rocks*. Bloom seems lost in thought. To explain this "trance," Stephen indulges in theosophic mumbo-jumbo. As if in rebuke, a passage couched in the historian Macaulay's vigorous matter-of-fact prose informs us that Bloom is merely contemplating "private transactions" of his own (1189). A debate begins and becomes a scientific disputation. Significantly, Bloom raises two of its topics: the determination of sex and infant mortality. Stephen's bitter blasphemy about the divine appetite for dead infants (1292) comes in for criticism.

Joyce parodies Dickens to comment on the happy birth ("Meanwhile the skill and patience of the physician...," 1310), and Walter Pater to render a memory of Bloom's, a game of bowls at Roundtown, with Stephen as a lad of four or five.[1] The sights of Stephen as a child and Bloom as a youth (1043), of course, belong properly to a chapter about birth and development. But Stephen is now full grown and no longer innocent. When the thunder sounds again he calls out the name of a pub, Burke's, to which they are all bound. Joyce uses a strenuous, consonant-chewing style modeled on Thomas Carlyle's to describe the roisterers' exit. As they go, they extravagantly praise Theodore Purefoy, father of the newborn. Now it is time to drink to the goddess of childbirth and loss of virginity ("*Per deam Partulam*...," 1439).

The long gestation is over, for child and for language. In the concluding pages Joyce makes his prose as up to date as possible. It is full of slang, Scottish and Irish and American black dialect, pidgin English, nonce words, babytalk, and drunken attempts to pronounce tongue-twisters ("The Leith police dismisseth us. The least tholice," 1565). From one point of view, this

---

1. Bloom has remembered this incident before in *Hades* (6.1010) when he thought about besting John Henry Menton at bowls.

is language at its worst. "The word" (1390), once sacred and generative, as at the opening of the gospel of John, is now fully degraded. But one could also regard language here as being at its most popular, playful, and free. With it we leave behind the literariness of the chapter's parodies and move among the common people. But we do not move into any clear narration of events. What seems to happen in Burke's, after Stephen pays for various potations, is that Bloom is identified as Molly's husband and Milly's father ("Photo's papli, by all that's gorgeous," 1535), the man in the macintosh appears, Mulligan disappears, and Stephen wonders where he will lay his head. Everyone talks about the major event of the day, the Gold Cup race, then about the forthcoming Gordon Bennett race for automobiles in Germany. At closing time Lynch and Stephen move off to Dublin's red-light district ("Change here for Bawdyhouse," 1572), Stephen being drunker than ever, on alcohol but also on the Latin phrases of his Catholic upbringing. *Laetabuntur in cubilibus suis*, he intones, "Let them sing aloud upon their beds," *Ut implerentur scripturae*, "that the scriptures may be fulfilled" (1574). Thus he prepares for a quasi-religious rite, as we will see in great detail in *Circe*. Finally, the last words in this chapter drunk on words come from an American evangelist. (Stephen and Lynch see his poster on display.) Putting the evangelist's just-folks exhortation ("The Deity aint no nickle dime bumshow," 1585) next to the solemn, thrice-repeated prayer which opened the chapter, we may judge just how much language has changed over the long years of its growth.

[15] *Circe* (pages 350–497)

This is the longest, strangest, and most ambitious chapter of *Ulysses*. It employs dialogue and interior monologue—conscious fantasies—but Joyce goes beyond these by now-familiar techniques to expose the *unconscious* minds of Stephen and Bloom. He dramatizes their repressed emotions. As the hour grows later and later, the two men, too drunk and too fatigued (respectively) to maintain their usual self-control, play out their deepest obsessions in grotesquely exaggerated form. They enjoy triumphs and suffer punishments their rational minds would never allow. They undergo instant and often highly comic metamorphoses. When Bloom recalls a visit to the Leopardstown racecourse, for instance, he dons, in fantasy, a sporting ensemble complete down to spats and billycock hat (536). Later, diagnosed

as a Mongoloid idiot, he gabbles in pidgin English (961). All this makes for
"good theater," and indeed *Circe*, unlike the novel as a whole, has been
successfully dramatized, as *Ulysses in Nighttown* (1958).

At the same time *Circe* serves Joyce by permitting virtuoso
transformations of language. As in *Oxen of the Sun* and *Sirens*, he forces
English words into new shapes. When Bloom feels deeply ambivalent, for
example, Joyce replaces his "No" and "Yes" with "Nes" and "Yo" (2766).
When he is distorted by concave and convex mirrors, Bloom emerges as
"Booloohoom" and *"jollypoldy"* (146). And the chapter brings back an extraordinary number of previous characters and themes for one more comic or
nightmarish turn. Among many other Dubliners, the Citizen from *Cyclops*,
Reuben J. Dodd from *Hades*, Gerty MacDowell from *Nausicaa*, Mrs Breen
from *Lestrygonians*, Myles Crawford from *Aeolus*, Ben Dollard from *Sirens*,
and Father Conmee from *Wandering Rocks* appear, all in new guises, as if
transformed by the power of Homer's enchantress Circe. The litany of the
Daughters of Erin ("Kidney of Bloom, pray for us...," 1940) summarizes
all the Bloomian chapters of the novel, so that we may remember what has
led up to the phantasmagoric events at the brothel.

Much of the anti-reality in *Circe* can confidently be ascribed to the
characters' minds. It makes sense that Stephen's imagination turns cancer
into a crab with green claws (4220). He knows, after all, that *cancer* is Latin
for "crab." But occasionally characters draw on knowledge which they
cannot have. In one fantasy sequence Bloom meets a domineering version
of Molly, who quotes "Nebrakada! Femininum!" (319); but that talismanic
phrase comes from a book which Stephen read, not Bloom (10.849). This
and other happenings in the chapter can only be explained by "magic."
Magic gives inanimate objects a voice and alters characters out of
recognition (Cissy Caffrey and Edy Boardman from *Nausicaa* appear as
whores). One task for the reader is to sort out the psychologically plausible
from the implausible, to distinguish the images generated by Bloom's self-
contempt and Stephen's guilt from the images generated by Joyce's own
inventiveness.

It is easy enough to summarize the actual events of the chapter. After
the drinking at Burke's pub, Mulligan slips away from Stephen, and the
latter wanders off drunkenly with Lynch to "nighttown," Dublin's red-light
district. Bloom follows Stephen (he is not sure why) to Bella Cohen's
brothel, enters, passes time innocently there, and observes with disapproval
the young man's helplessness about money. The customers and the whores

dance. Stephen swings wildly with his stick at a nightmare vision of his dead mother, then rushes outside, only to become embroiled in an argument with two drunk and pugnacious British soldiers. One of them eventually hits Stephen, knocking him unconscious. Bloom stands guard over the young man: the sonless father and the fatherless son find themselves alone for the first time in the novel.

This story sticks close indeed to the one told in the *Odyssey*, where Ulysses, protected by the magic herb "moly," rescues his men from Circe, who has feasted them and turned them into swine. Ulysses sails for home but not before enjoying the enchantress' favors for a full year. A long literary tradition interpreted the *Circe* story as an allegory of lust, which has the power to turn men into beasts. No doubt Joyce knew of this tradition, since he depicts "male brutes" as drugged animals roaring *"in their loosebox"* (2019), but he scarcely makes Bloom and Stephen thralls to lust. Certainly Joyce knew of and imitated other literary stories of sexuality and hallucination. *Circe* adopts some details from the nightmare visions of Flaubert's *Temptation of St Anthony* and others, especially at the beginning, from the fantastic Walpurgisnacht scene in Goethe's *Faust* (the "will-o'-the-wisps" in the first stage direction, for example, come from *Faust*).

*   *   *

The first few pages of the chapter illustrate Circe's transforming power. On every side we glimpse deformation and animality ("idiot," "palsied," "pigmy," "bandy," "gnome," "lair"). Through random insults and drunken songs Stephen and Lynch pass into nighttown. The former chants Latin "with joy" in a parody of the Mass, then carries on with a few esthetic speculations. Perhaps gestures should replace language, he comments. Stephen obviously savors the blasphemy of what he is doing—philosophizing in the slums, sinning deliberately, substituting "deam" (goddess) for "deum" (god) in one mock response (122). Bloom blasphemes in his own way, buying an unkosher "crubeen" (pigsfoot) and a sheep's trotter. A tram barely misses him, leading to thoughts about exercise. At this point (199) he is still cautious. Beginning with the sudden appearance of Bloom's father Rudolph we witness a long series of accusations against our hero, who no doubts feels guilty simply for being in nighttown. Rudolph Bloom claws Leopold's face, replicating the recognition scene in *Leah* about which we heard in *Lotus Eaters* (201), and anticipating a second parent-son meeting in this chapter. Then Bloom's mother Ellen materializes to shake her head over her youthful son's muddied clothes. The next accuser is Molly ("Marion," in Turkish costume), who teases him with a line adapted from her *Don Giovanni* duet, "*Ti trema un poco il cuore?*" (351). Doesn't Bloom's heart tremble a little for his wife? After a real-life bawd accosts him, an imagined Gerty does so. She loves being degraded, like Bloom himself. Then Bloom's old flame Mrs Breen teases and flirts with him, gently, making up for Marion's disdain. They play the "teapot" game, substituting that word for another one (here, "burning") which has to be guessed.

We leave the pleasant old memories for the reality of obscene invitations from whores and a crude tale about someone defecating into the bucket of porter left for some plasterers (585). Bloom's "Coincidence too" (592) seems to implicate him in this or a similar misdeed. Now, in nighttown, he wonders if he is on a wildgoose chase. Cursing his own absurdity, he gives the dog who has been trailing him the crubeen and trotter, only to be interrogated by the police, "the Watch." They decline the grammatical cases of "Bloom," ending with the accusative (677). Desperately Bloom thinks of alibis and excuses. He offers Molly as a bribe and tries in vain to pronounce the Biblical password "shibboleth" (770). He tries a Masonic sign. With each of Bloom's pretensions to respectability, appropriate debunkers appear, as when "Well, I follow a literary occupation" (801) produces Myles Crawford, then Philip Beaufoy scorning Bloom's writerly ambitions. By now we are in an imaginary court. The scullerymaid Mary Driscoll accuses Bloom of an assault, and Bloom's counsel, the has-been J. J. O'Molloy, pleads first mental deficiency, then conspiracy ("When in doubt persecute Bloom," 975). Bloom claims to belong to high society, but then high society attacks him in the guise of well-to-do ladies testifying to his obscene interest in them (here, Joyce draws on Leopold von Sacher Masoch's lurid novel *Venus in Furs*). For example, Mrs Yelverton Barry denounces his invitation to misconduct herself with him at 4:30 on a Thursday—the exact time, of course, of Molly and Boylan's assignation. By such a mental feat Bloom the sinned against disguises himself as Bloom the sinner. And the sinner quickly offers himself as victim. The ladies promise Bloom a horsewhipping, making him cringe in pleasure and pain. Their ultimate charge against him? "He is a wellknown cuckold" (1117). Jingling bed quoits and cuckoo clock supply the sound effects of cuckoldry. A jury of Bloom's Dublin enemies appears.

Death threatens, as Bloom is sentenced to hang, and Paddy Dignam's wasted spirit becomes visible.

Two numbered discs from Tom Rochford's machine wobble, signaling the end of a music hall turn and reminding us that *Circe* is among other things a series of fantastic theatrical "acts," comic, sentimental, acrobatic (1265), magical. Momentarily we return to reality. Bloom halts outside the brothel, guided there by the sound of church music from inside. The whore with whom he flirts, Zoe, asks him if he is Stephen's father. She also takes away his lucky potato, depriving our modern Ulysses of his moly. To find a more significant Bloomian safeguard, however, we have only to add an "l" to the Greek word, producing "Molly"; Zoe cannot deprive Bloom of his husbandly regard—love not unmixed with fear—for his wife, which is why the whore succeeds only in flirting with him. In Bloom's brief reverie Zoe murmurs the Hebrew words from the Song of Songs meaning "I am black but comely, ye daughters of Jerusalem" (1333). Thus the Orient continues to cast its mysterious spell over Bloom, but as always in *Ulysses*, banality lies folded in mystery. Zoe's breath smells of garlic, and the "roses" of her lips draw apart to reveal "*a sepulchre of the gold of kings and their mouldering bones*" (1341)—i.e., the fillings in her teeth.

The next seventeen pages of the chapter last only a second of real time but enact a gigantic mental drama of Bloomian rise and fall. Responding to Bloom's swaggering talk about smoking, Zoe tells him to make "a stump speech out of it" (1352), thereby launching us into political fantasy. All goes well at first. Elected lord mayor of Dublin, cheered on in Irish and Hebrew, welcomed in a huge parade, acknowledged as Parnell's successor by his brother, Bloom is acclaimed in rapid succession "the world's greatest reformer" (1459) and "very puissant ruler of this realm" (1472). He repudiates Molly, proclaims the New Bloomusalem, deals summarily with "M'Intosh's" charge against him, and in one of Joyce's funniest paragraphs plays the role of consummate politician (1600). Then like Solomon he renders wise judgment. Alas, accusations grow more frequent and vicious, and the mob turns on him exactly as it turned on Parnell (1761). Bloom's defence? Doctor Mulligan pronounces him a virgin, Doctor Dixon a mother-to-be. He gives birth and performs other miracles but to no avail. Fellow Jews make him a scapegoat while Christians burn him alive. Bloom is "carbonised" as a result, which is the link back to actuality when Zoe says "Talk away till you're black in the face" (1959).

The whore draws Bloom inside, where Kitty and Fanny are entertaining Lynch and Stephen. More animal terms ("boa," "catterpillar," "snakes") recall the original Circe's palace. Somewhat incoherently, Stephen discourses on church music and on musical technique. He is fascinated by the interval of the fifth because it calls for a "return" to the octave, by the octave because it suggests a kind of identity; thus he harps on his private themes of return and identity. Outside, a gramophone blares "The Holy City" and confused fantasies about Apocalypse follow. The whores confess their pasts; in a travesty of theosophy, a Celtic god appears uttering Sanskrit warnings (2268). Back to reality, very briefly, before Virag Lipoti, a grotesque version of Bloom's grandfather, enters. He chastises Bloom, as the father Rudolph did, but more violently (and obscurely), and he moves in spasms. Is he subject, perhaps, to the "Locomotor ataxy" Florry mentions (2591)? For that matter everyone in this chapter, including Bloom (2023), has trouble moving. Sometimes the Protean Virag talks like a mad scientist, but he also gobbles like a turkey (one of many animal transformations) and quotes music-hall songs; it is not easy to make consistent symbolic sense of him or trace him to the obsessions of Bloom's unconscious mind. Possibly he represents Bloom's sceptical, cynical side, the side which might doubt Jesus' divinity and accuse Mary of misbehaving with Panther, a Roman centurion (2599). If Virag stands for cynicism, then Henry Flower, who also appears in these pages (2478), may stand for Bloom's sentimentality.

Joyce's attention now shifts to Stephen. Florry wants him to sing, and the terms of his refusal make her suspect he is "out of Maynooth," a seminary student. He is indeed "out" of Maynooth and Catholicism now, Stephen comments (2535). Two sides of Stephen, prudent ("Philip Sober") and reckless ("Philip Drunk") contend for mastery of the young man. We hear of a priestly customer of the whores.

Through these pages Joyce alternates between strange interjections from Virag and the two Philips and ordinary brothel conversation ("And Mary Shortall that was in the lock with the pox," 2578).[1] Florry, sure that Stephen is a spoiled priest or a monk (2649), provokes an appearance of Stephen as cardinal, primate of Ireland ("monk" and "primate" result in his

---

1. Perhaps not entirely ordinary conversation. Kitty's comment on Mary Shortall supplies a blasphemous version of the Holy Family, with a poxy Mary, a holy ghost ("Jimmy Pidgeon"), and a child smothered with convulsions. See Blamires, *The New Bloomsday Book*, p. 172.

acolytes being "simian"). Unable to stop thinking about the prelate he might have become, Stephen yet pictures himself as only a comedy cardinal with a rosary of corks.

A male customer leaves and the fearsome madam Bella Cohen enters. Her line about being all in a sweat (2750) is literally spoken and succeeded by an equally literal "You'll know me the next time" (3481). But in between comes an imagined scene of Bloomian humiliation. With desire and with reluctance he craves her domination, or "his" domination since Bella soon becomes Bello.[1] Bloom, "she," sinks to the floor, an animal about to be mastered. In every possible way Bloom suffers, physically and psychologically. Every sexual fantasy he has entertained in the past is brought up against him—his liking for women's clothes, for instance, which now leads to his being treated as a maid of all work (3086) and then as a pampered, perfumed whore. More and more clearly we understand that Bloom's own guilty mind, in the guise of Bello, is attacking him for complaisance in Molly's affair. "Can you do a man's job?" he is asked (3132). In a further torment, Bello describes Molly and Blazes' lovemaking for Bloom, graphically. A new, softer-voiced attacker appears in the form of the nymph from the framed picture above the Blooms' bed at 7 Eccles Street. Bloom rescued her from the unsavory company of contraceptive ads in the magazine *Photo Bits*...but what sights she has seen! What snoring and farting from Bloom she has heard! And worse sounds: chamber-pot sounds, metamorphosed into the sound of an Irish waterfall ("Poulaphouca," 3299). The nymph and the yews (from the brothel wallpaper) have witnessed Bloom's adolescent "infamy"—masturbation, presumably. Turning the tables on his attackers, Bloom accuses the nymph, now costumed as a nun, of being "Shy but willing" (3450).

In the brothel Bloom and Bella trade insults. He has recovered his self-esteem along with his potato, and as if protected by that talisman, he gets Stephen's money back when the young man overpays. He agrees to hold all of Stephen's money. Zoe reads palms, finding in Stephen's courage, femininity, and the promise of a meeting with someone. The stray sentence "I see it in your face" (3663) produces a hallucination of Father Dolan, who in *A Portrait of the Artist* saw laziness in the young Stephen's face and struck him on the hand. As for the lines on Bloom's hand, they identify him as a

---

1. As we have clearly seen, mannish women fascinate Bloom, but perhaps we may trace the Bella-Bello metamorphosis to something specific: Mrs Bandmann Palmer's *en travesti* performance as Hamlet on the night of June 15 (5.194).

henpecked husband. To confirm his marital shortcomings, an imagined car bearing Boylan arrives. Wearing the cuckold's horns, Bloom witnesses the lovemaking with mingled excitement and abhorrence ("Show! Hide!", 3815). Shakespeare, a second cuckold according to Stephen, mentions a putative third, Othello or "Oldfellow" (3828).

Asked to demonstrate French ("parleyvoo"), Stephen replies with a wonderful parody of Gallic naughtiness. His father appears, then a racing crowd, then Mr Deasy on horseback. Snatches of "My Girl's a Yorkshire Girl" come through the window and Zoe wants them all to dance. They do so, with music from the pianola and under the imagined direction of the dancing master Maginni. Appropriately costumed girls from Ponchielli's *Dance of the Hours* join the weaving and unweaving patterns, which grow more and more frenzied, until finally Stephen is giddy. So is Joyce's prose, with its breathless, dizzying syntax. Simon Dedalus appears abruptly with a warning against his wife's family, and at the same moment Stephen thinks "Dance of death" (4139). At this dramatic juncture the mother appears, beastly dead, breathing mortality on her son. She urges him to repent and reminds him of the pity she has felt. With his ashplant stick Stephen defends himself against her religion and her suffocating love; heroically, he smashes the brothel chandelier, calling out "Nothung," the name of the Wagnerian hero Siegfried's sword. Then he rushes out, unheroically, leaving Bloom to placate an angry Bella.

Bloom pursues Stephen, and a huge imaginary crowd including all the major characters of the novel follows him. At the corner Stephen elaborately patronizes the drunk British soldiers, Privates Carr and Compton, who think Stephen has somehow insulted Cissy (4394). A man of peace, like Bloom in *Cyclops*, Stephen knows he can strive against religious and political tyranny, priest and king, only mentally (4436). Nevertheless he and the privates are urged on to the fight. Lord Tennyson, Dolly Gray (heroine of a Boer War song), and some of the crowd champion the soldiers; the Irish exiles or "wild geese" Kevin Egan and Don Emile, the Citizen, the Croppy Boy, and Old Gummy Granny urge Stephen to stand up for Ireland. Edward VII impartially wishes both men the best of luck. Only Bloom works for peace. Momentarily interrupting the argument (and building up suspense), Joyce describes a conflagration, an earthquake, an apocalyptic battle, and a fantasy black mass complete with blasphemies and reversals, including reversals of letters (4708). Perhaps we should ascribe all of this to Stephen's fevered egotism, which here as elsewhere dramatizes his doings. After all, the Crucifixion was accompanied by cosmic disturbances...why not this altercation in nighttown? To strengthen the Stephen-Christ parallel, Lynch earns the title of "Judas" by refusing to help his friend (4730). Finally Carr is enraged enough to strike, and Stephen falls unconscious to the ground. The Watch arrive, and in spite of Bloom's efforts it seems that they will take Stephen's name, but at the last moment Corny Kelleher gets them to drop the matter (earlier in the novel he has been thought to be in cahoots with the police). Kelleher and Bloom still have to explain to each other their being in nighttown, and they do so, elaborately and falsely, earning a horselaugh (4879). Off Kelleher goes.

Father Bloom tries to wake son Dedalus, but Stephen mutters a few words—black panther, vampire, a snatch of the Yeats poem he sang for his mother—and lapses back into unconsciousness. After all the effects this chapter has provided, it seems impossible that Joyce could produce a new one for the end, and yet he does so. He gives Bloom a serene interlude of understanding and misunderstanding. The older man communes with the night, thinking with pity of Stephen's wasted education and with practicality of a girl who might look after Stephen (he has misheard "Fergus" as "Ferguson"). At this solemn moment phrases of Masonic rite come to his mind ("swear that I will always hail," 4951). So do mysterious words about the tide and the sands of the sea. Is he thinking of Sandymount strand, where both he and Stephen walked and meditated? Whatever his thoughts, Bloom stands loyally on guard and is rewarded by a last vision of his dead son Rudy at the age of eleven years. Costumed as a fairy changeling, Rudy is perfect and wholly unreal, the creation of paternal sentimentality. Unlike all the projections of guilt in the chapter, who were entirely willing to castigate Bloom, this projection of love stays silent and apart. Rudy smiles as he reads his Hebrew text (we know it is Hebrew because he reads from right to left) but gazes unseeing into his father's wonderstruck eyes.

[16] *Eumaeus* (pages 501–543)

After the excitements of *Circe*, we need a change, and we get one in *Eumaeus*. In this deliberately prosaic chapter ordinary actions replace hallucinatory transformations, and narration replaces mental drama. We see the characters from the outside and are simply told their thoughts, in such straightforward formulations as "Stephen thought to think of Ibsen..."

(52). Interior monologue is nowhere employed. Everything is real. The Dublin United Tramways Company sandstrewer is just that, not a beast bearing down on Bloom, a "dragon," as it was in *Circe*. The style of the chapter is perhaps all too real, a collection of clichés such as might plausibly be spoken by someone too tired to be original. On and on the hackneyed phrases go ("yeoman service," "not to put too fine a point on it," "as luck would have it"). They create a late night world in which Bloom and Stephen seem trapped, as they mark time, waiting for Stephen to recover from his drunkenness and his "fight" with the soldiers. Joyce has also made the narrative of the chapter laboriously fussy, devoting it to finicking corrections, elegant variations, unnecessary explanations, and circumlocution. The prose sounds like an exaggeration of Bloom's own speaking style: "I met your respected father on a recent occasion…today in fact, or to be strictly accurate, on yesterday" (254). The older man unquestionably fusses about Stephen, giving him advice and keeping him sober. No doubt he is somewhat nervous about acting the orthodox Samaritan, the surrogate father.

*   *   *

Having been "bucked up," Stephen sets off with Bloom to a cabman's shelter, where they will be able to get something non-alcoholic to drink. Securing no cab, they walk. At Store Street, Stephen (the man of the mind) thinks of Ibsen, while Bloom (the man of the body) smells baking bread; they will be contrasted in various ways throughout the chapter, and in the next one as well. "Lord John" Corley accosts Stephen, begging. Knowing misery himself, as the Latin tag "*haud ignarus…*" (misquoted from the *Aeneid*) says, Stephen feels sorry for Corley and gives him a halfcrown, thus immediately disregarding the warning about "squandermania" (87) he has just gotten. Bloom thinks Stephen might go home to his father's house, but Stephen, remembering his sisters' misery there, knows better. Mulligan, certainly, cannot be trusted. Bloom no sooner commits himself to this judgment than he pulls cautiously back, acknowledging Dr Mulligan's talents.

After passing some Italians arguing violently about not being paid enough money, the two men enter the shelter. The clichés here are foreign ones, as if the style were infected by the foreign language just overheard. The cabman's shelter stands in for the hut of the swineherd Eumaeus in the

Odyssey, the site of the long-awaited meeting between Ulysses and Telemachus, father and son. In Homer, the two Greeks plot their revenge against the usurping suitors. In Joyce, the two Irishmen move more circuitously to a partial understanding of each other. The Dublin Eumaeus, meanwhile, is James Fitzharris, "Skin-the-Goat," an Invincible or Fenian once imprisoned for complicity in the Phoenix Park murders. He serves Stephen coffee and a roll. An old sailor named Murphy, an arrival on the ship *Rosevean* which Stephen beheld at the end of *Proteus*, begins telling them a series of highly improbable travel tales. This, too, is Homeric, since Ulysses told Eumaeus false but revealing stories about himself as a sea-rover. Murphy, Ulysses, Sinbad the sailor (858), the flying Dutchman (861)—all have wandered over the sea. *Eumaeus* makes much of wandering, and much of coming home too; Murphy has a waiting wife in Queenstown. There are "Quite a number of stories" on that topic (424), Bloom acknowledges, and adds the names Rip Van Winkle (who was forgotten by everyone) and Enoch Arden (who found his wife married to someone else) to the list. With these fictions he secretly admits, and counters, his worst fears of marital betrayal.

Though suspicious of Murphy, Bloom thinks longingly of sea travel. Perhaps he could arrange a tour for the "Tweedy-Flower grand opera company" (525); this is his own false but revealing story. He considers the advantages of travel, while the old sailor tells them all about Italians and stilettos. Has he seen Gibraltar? Bloom asks. But the sailor has nothing to convey about Molly's native place. Murphy displays a tattoo with the number 16, hinting at a homosexual relation to the young man pictured. A street-walker looks in, embarrassing Bloom because she has accosted him before and apparently knows Molly (11.1252). "Unfortunate creature!" he exclaims (731) but, for Stephen's benefit, does not omit a lecture on the evils of prostitution. Stephen finds other kinds of selling worse. The two exchange opinions on the soul and the existence of God, Stephen blaspheming, Bloom championing science. It is clear that the older man enjoys this intellectual interchange, even if Stephen's comments tend to be short and cryptic; clear also that Bloom fails to understand just what these comments mean. Bloom continues to doubt the sailor's truthfulness, but after all, he says, Italians are hotblooded...like Spaniards. Somewhat clumsily he drags in Molly and her Spanish heritage, as if determined to make her passionate temperament (873) known to Stephen.

Skin-the-Goat, a less eloquent version of the Citizen, delivers a speech about Irish resources and the coming collapse of England. An argument with Murphy follows, while Bloom contemplates the possibility of Irish independence. Characteristically, he goes back and forth in his thinking, cautiously worrying about police informers, then admiring a man "who had actually brandished a knife" (1058). Later he will insist on looking "at both sides of the question" (1094). After a digression about murder and adultery (is Bloom momentarily thinking of himself as a wronged husband who might brandish a knife?), he reports to Stephen on his encounter with the Citizen. Interestingly enough, Bloom now downplays his Jewishness ("though in reality I'm not," 1085), while he exaggerates his effect on the Citizen. But he speaks the truth when he claims to resent violence and intolerance. Stephen responds to all this by quoting the Vulgate Bible (*Ex quibus*, Romans 9:5) on the Jewish origin of Christ. In a long speech, for him, Bloom defends the Jews ("they") and proposes a sort of socialism. Everyone who works should be given a "tidysized income" (1134). But Stephen will not work. What would be the point of work in Ireland, the *faubourg Saint Patrice* or St Patrick's suburb? "Ireland must be important because it belongs to me" (1164), he adds, a hyperbole which mystifies Bloom. Rebuked, the older man falls silent and worries about the enigmatic young man before him, and about the decline in modern morals. In an important paragraph beginning "For which and further reasons" (1216), he nevertheless resolves to do what he can.

Bloom reads aloud Paddy Dignam's obituary from the *Telegraph*. One last insult left over from the funeral is that his name has been misspelled. Mr Deasy's letter also appears in print, and an account of the Gold Cup. After a cabman's sudden comment on Parnell, Bloom ruminates on that Irish hero. No chance of his returning, our skeptic thinks. He remembers handing the great man's hat back to him and remembers too Parnell's love affair with Kitty O'Shea—a case of a "real man" replacing a husband not "up to the scratch" (1380). All this makes Bloom wonder if love can exist between married folk. By guessing that Kitty had Spanish blood, Bloom partially excuses her, and of course excuses Molly as well. He now shows Stephen a postcard of Molly, in the full bloom of womanhood; obviously he wants Stephen to drink in her beauty. He even seems to want Stephen to imagine an affair with Molly. Better a still attractive married woman than profligate women who might give him a "nice dose" of venereal disease (1555).

It would be risky to invite Stephen home to 7 Eccles Street, Bloom thinks, but on the other hand the young man needs something nutritious. He proposes cocoa. Off they go into the night air, and Stephen asks an uncharacteristically child-like question about upside-down café chairs. To this Bloom gives a characteristically practical answer and, acting like a parent, takes Stephen's arm. The young man feels the strangeness of the older man's touch yet does not pull away. He has changed since the opening scene of the novel, when he carefully disengaged himself from Mulligan's arm and Mulligan's offered friendship.

On the way to Eccles Street each man speaks of the music he likes, Bloom favoring light classics and the Rossini *Stabat Mater* which Molly sang so thrillingly, Stephen the more recherché songs of the Elizabethans. They pass a horse, which provides one last opportunity for Bloomian thoughts of kindness to animals, and Stephen sings an old song: "Von der Sirenen... From the Sirens' craftiness Poets make poems" (1815). A "phenomenally beautiful tenor voice," Bloom judges (1820). Stephen could be a successful concert artist, if only he had someone to look after him, manage his clothes ...Bloom is full of hope and good advice and undeterred by down-to-earth Dublin reality in the form of horse droppings on the street. Bloom and Stephen, the full figure and the lean, enjoying what the narrator in his hackneyed manner calls a *"tête à tête"* about Sirens and usurpers, finish the chapter to the strains of the Irish song "The Low-Backed Car."

[17] *Ithaca* (pages 544–607)

No one would have trouble guessing that the art of this chapter, as recorded in the outline of *Ulysses* Joyce gave Stuart Gilbert, is "science." The severely impersonal questions and answers of *Ithaca* seem part of an objective, fact-seeking, scientific inquiry, an inquiry bent on conveying as much exact information as possible. We are informed (110) that Bloom lights a gasflame of 14 candlepower, no more, no less; the volumes on his bookshelves are painstakingly catalogued for us, right down to details of their bindings (1361). As if afraid to jump to conclusions too quickly, the chapter's style describes things without naming them, so that an ordinary clothesline appears as "a curvilinear rope, stretched between two holdfasts" (150). As if afraid to leave out anything potentially significant, the style obsessively lists particulars: addresses, dates, locations, names. The style

outdoes the scientific curiosity of Bloom, multiplying and (usually) getting
right the facts which he has so often gotten wrong during the day. But in its
intellectually disciplined questioning and answering, *Ithaca* also suggests a
debate on esthetic theory or a catechism, and therefore Stephen. The two
men share the chapter equally. Over and over, with evenhanded precision, it
records their similarities and differences.

Precise the chapter may be, but it is also comic. Perhaps a slightly mad
scientist is running its inquiries, or a scientist led astray by fascination with
his method. The lists and catalogues are ludicrously extensive, in the mode
of *Cyclops*; comparisons are carried out to insane length, as in the
arithmetical meditation on Bloom's and Stephen's ages (447; Joyce's math,
incidentally, is all wrong). Prose objectivity occasionally lapses into poetic
playfulness, as in "with thought of aught he sought though fraught with
nought" (285) or an examination of the schooling of "Stoom" and
"Blephen" (549). Like a number of previous chapters, *Ithaca* establishes a
rhetorical mode and then trips over it. Rarely, it vaults over it, achieving a
real if mysterious poetry. No passage in *Ulysses* is more eloquent, more
"Joycean," than an imaginative and rhythmical speculation in *Ithaca* on the
affinity between moon and woman (1159).

Toward the end of the *Odyssey*, Homer's hero, together with his son,
enters his palace on the island of Ithaca to kill the suitors. Joyce contrives a
number of resemblances between the returning Ulysses and the returning
Bloom. (Both men enter their houses by a stratagem, for instance.) But he
makes nothing of the slaughter of suitors, Bloom being a man of peace.
What abundantly interests Joyce is the recovery of place and possessions.
He allows Bloom to recover his "kingdom," 7 Eccles Street, he inventories
the contents of the kitchen, and he shows us Bloom's daydream of a
grander home, "Bloom Cottage" or "Saint Leopold's" (1580). Meanwhile
Bloom and Stephen inventory the day they have gone through, taking
possession of June 16, 1904. *Ithaca* rehearses many events of the novel
(sometimes making them clearer) and at one or two important points
provides general summations ("His mood?", 348). Joyce may have been
tempted to summation because this chapter, though placed next-to-last in
the finished novel, was the last one he wrote.

*   *   *

As *Ithaca* begins, Stephen and Bloom walk through Dublin streets (their exact itinerary is given, of course) to Bloom's house. Having no key, Bloom enters by the "area," the open space in front of the basement kitchen, admits Stephen, lights a fire, and washes. Stephen does not wash, disliking both literal water and figurative "aquacities of thought and language" (240). They drink cocoa. Joyce's father and son sit comfortably enough together, but they are not so intimate as Ulysses and Telemachus. At one point Bloom thinks, erroneously, that Stephen is engaged in "mental composition" (384). The hint of literature leads to information about Bloom's own past writings, and then to information about each man's past, their incidental points of contact, their parents, and their baptisms. Bloom has undergone three, we learn. He has also entertained many ideas about useful inventions and effective ads, and about ways of keeping Molly occupied, such as "courses of evening instruction" (672). Throughout these pages the older man passes images and ideas on to the younger, who translates them into the forms of his own loneliness and sometimes gives them back again. For example, Bloom's idea of a transparent showcart with two smartly dressed office girls (608) allows Stephen to construct a melancholy dramatic scene—like something out of Ibsen—between a young man and a young woman. Restless, sighing, this young woman writes over and over again the enigmatic message "Queen's Hotel." The name can suggest to Bloom only the place of his father's lonely suicide. A mere "Coincidence" of homonymity, he decides (633). Joyce's point is not so much the coincidental "Queen's Hotel" as the imperfect coinciding of his characters. They share a name or an image but only in a way demonstrating that what they chiefly share is isolation; their messages to each other remain enigmatic.

Passing to matters of the mind, in a lighter mood, Stephen and Bloom discuss Aristotle, Jewish intellectuals, the Hebrew and Irish languages. They write characters on a blank page of *Sweets of Sin*, Bloom managing to keep the embarrassing title hidden. They sing for each other, Bloom the Zionist anthem "Hatikvah" ("*Kolod balejwaw...*", 763), Stephen a ballad accusing a Jewish daughter of the murder of a little Christian boy. Stephen seems to identify himself with this youth led "to a secret infidel apartment" (836). Bloom himself has a daughter, and he recalls Milly at various ages. She resembles the cat, who will return from roaming. Will Milly? Feeling vicariously paternal, Bloom offers Stephen a place to sleep. This is an offer with such advantages as seclusion for the guest, intellectual stimulation for the host, and improved Italian pronunciation for the hostess, Molly, but Stephen gratefully declines, as Bloom once declined an offer from the youthful Stephen (475). Possibly the two men agree that Stephen and Molly will exchange Italian lessons for singing lessons (962), though the all-inclusive prose makes it difficult to know exactly what has been accepted, what declined.

They go outside together, passing the entering cat, chanting a psalm,[1] to see a "heaventree" of stars (1039). In the garden, Bloom points out constellations and thinks deep thoughts of space, time, and nature. He is unwilling to disbelieve in astrological influences and convinced by the affinity of moon and woman. The older and the younger man urinate companionably together while entertaining very different thoughts, just as, a moment later, they translate the pealing bell of St George's church into very different terms (1230). Stephen departs. Now alone, Bloom remembers other departed friends and another witnessed dawn from his youth. Breathing deeply, he goes back inside, bumping his head on the sideboard, which has been moved. A description of furniture follows, with hints of what Molly and Boylan have been up to (a copy of "Love's Old Sweet Song" sits on the piano). Bloom lights incense and, taking stock of himself, gazes in the mirror. There follows the taking stock of his books and, after a partial undressing, a budget, the accounting of Bloom's expenditures during the day. (This document fails to record the money left behind at the brothel.) In abundant detail we hear of Bloom's dream residence, which he wishes to purchase, not inherit. This "Bloom Cottage," a masterwork of his bourgeois imagination, boasts every high-class furnishing and modern convenience, and it requires a grander Bloom to live in it—a landed gentleman, a justice of the peace (1610)—not to mention some grandiose schemes to make money to pay for it (1674).

Back in the reality of 7 Eccles Street, we are shown the (revealing) contents of a drawer, to which Bloom now adds his letter from Martha. He reflects pleasantly on encounters with females during the day, but a second drawer containing memorabilia of Rudolph Bloom makes him melancholy. He has been no pious Jew to please a father. Protected by inherited funds,

---

1. In English Bibles, Psalm 114: "When Israel went forth from Egypt, the house of Jacob from a people of strange language..." Both men go out of "the house of bondage" mentioned in the psalm, but Bloom will go back into it, as his mental slip in *Aeolus* has predicted.

Bloom need not fear poverty, but Joyce nevertheless provides a speculation on poverty and the means of avoiding it, death or departure. Should Bloom depart Dublin, without Molly? There are arguments on both sides, but finally the advantages of an occupied bed and Molly's ample bedwarmed flesh prevail. Bloom recapitulates, in terms borrowed from religion, the events of the day, ponders enigmas (who was M'Intosh?), rehearses his failures, notes Molly's underwear, puts on his nightshirt, and enters the bed.

Bloom imagines those who have preceded him there (2132)—this is not necessarily an accurate list of Molly's actual lovers—and thinks with mixed feelings of the last of the series, Boylan. Retribution? Never, Bloom decides. He kisses Molly's bottom, waking her, and replies to her sleepy questions, leaving out a few details (Martha, Gerty, the argument with the Citizen) of what he has done. We learn, finally and definitively, that Bloom and Molly have not enjoyed normal conjugal relations for ten years; nor have they enjoyed normal mental intercourse since Milly's puberty, at which point mother and daughter joined together to interrogate Bloom, limiting his freedom. As Bloom and Molly converse more laconically and the episode nears its end, the narration seems to pull back from the pair. Joyce views his characters from an ever-greater distance, invoking latitude and longitude to locate them, watching them move through space with the moving earth, and viewing them also as mythic figures who have moved in time. Molly is the earth-goddess Gea-Tellus, Bloom "the childman weary." He has traveled indeed. On the last page Joyce sends his Ulysses, his Sinbad the Sailor, off to sleep with a lullaby. The scientific style yields to melodious calming nonsense. A chapter full of information, though not of resolution—we know hardly anything about what is going to happen—closes with a black dot.

[18] *Penelope* (pages 608–644)

For the last chapter Joyce returns to interior monologue, the essential technique of all the early chapters, thus coming back to his starting point. Moreover he returns to a character about whom we have been hearing since *Calypso*, giving her, for the first time, a chance to think and not be thought about. In eight vast sentences of freely associated memories, speculations, and exclamations Molly Bloom reveals herself. Like Gerty MacDowell, she is an imaginative bringer-together rather than a logical separator (as "Im" and "hed" show, she outdoes Gerty by bringing together the letters of contractions and by disdaining marks of punctuation). She circles widely, moving with complete freedom through space and time, but in the end she keeps coming back to favorable or unfavorable contemplation of Bloom, the man in bed beside her. She never forgets him. In this sense, if in no other, Molly the faithless wife resembles Homer's faithful Penelope.

*   *   *

Following Molly through her sentences entails tracing her movements from one idea to another. These movements are by no means arbitrary. At the start, for instance, her somewhat indignant knowledge that Bloom has asked for breakfast in bed brings back a time when he pretended to be sick in order to please Mrs Riordan (Stephen's "Aunt" Dante). The old woman's remembered miserliness and censorious chatter make Molly scornful about all prudish women. Ever down-to-earth ("I suppose she was pious because no man would look at her twice," 10), Molly wonders that Mrs Riordan did not want other women to cover their faces. (Molly herself has appeared, in Bloom's imagination, with a yashmak or veil covering her face: 15.359.) Even Bloom was probably glad to leave Mrs Riordan and her dog behind, she thinks, and suddenly, after much contempt for her husband ("doing his highness"), she admits that she admires his politeness. Consistency of judgment is not something she cares about. But Molly is neither ignorant nor unintelligent. She knows about the smutty photograph of a nun he keeps in a drawer; she knows that he has met other women this past night, though she can only guess who they might be. "Yes," she keeps thinking to herself, confirming her own understanding of the world (and men). "Yes" also confirms her acceptance of that world. Molly is no denier. Joyce described her as "the flesh that always says yes."[1]

At the beginning, one opinion she decidedly says "yes" to is that men, all men, are "weak and puling when theyre sick," whereas women hide things so as not to give trouble (34). In general, she does not think much of men, with their selfishness, their vulgarity, their intellectual pretensions. In particular, she does not think much of Bloom's sexual activity, now or in the past, when he was excited by Mary the scullerymaid, the same "Mary" who accuses Bloom in *Circe*. When she contemplates sexuality, she

---

1. *Letters of James Joyce* I, 170.

recognizes that in spite of all the talk about it "its just the ordinary," a normal part of living, and yet without a pause she begins to long for "a kiss long and hot" (106). Was "he" satisfied with her? she wonders, and the context makes it clear that she means Boylan (often Molly's "he's" are ambiguous). As she will think more than once, she disliked Boylan's slapping her behind, as though she were an animal. In her memory Boylan is something of an animal himself, a "Stallion" with a determined vicious look in his eye (152). A thunderclap wakened Molly from her post-coital nap and terrified her, just as thunder earlier terrified Stephen in *Oxen of the Sun*. In her momentary guilt about the adultery, Molly said a Hail Mary—at which Bloom, with his belief in "grey matter" rather than the human soul, would scoff.

She wonders if Bloom has been with Josie Powell (Mrs Breen), then mixes catty thoughts of the two together with recollections of Bloom's proposal to her ("I had the devils own job to get it out of him," 196). With all his faults Poldy is vastly superior to Mr Breen: he always wipes his feet and takes off his hat. Back to thoughts of Boylan, from whom Molly plans to get a ring with an aquamarine (262), and to a memory of an earlier admirer, the tenor Bartell d'Arcy, who kissed her in a church. Nothing so terrible about that, she concludes. Back to Bloom. Molly knows all about his fascinated interest in underwear and his taste for writing dirty words in letters, but she also knows he has brains. She grows nostalgic for a moment—once, Bloom wrote her letters twice a day and sent her eight big poppies—but only for a moment. She turns away from the past to the future and hopes Boylan will come again on Monday. She hopes also he will buy her presents in Belfast. She'd better get money out of him, since he's not the marrying kind. Another man from the past comes to mind, Lieutenant Gardner, a "lovely fellow in khaki," who died in the Boer War (390). Throughout these pages Molly moves rapidly from one man to another: d'Arcy, Gardner, Boylan with his natty clothes and his anger about the Gold Cup race, and always Bloom.

Molly thinks that she will have to diet (450). Unlike her husband, she is naturally expansive and generous, with herself and others. Bloom ought to quit his *Freeman* job and get something higher-paying. She knows how attracted to her Joe Cuffe was when she tried to patch up his quarrel with Bloom, and she knows how attracted to her breasts Boylan was this afternoon. For his part, Bloom once eased her milk-swollen breasts by sucking them, then reported on the taste of the milk. If Molly could only collect the astonishing things he says (580)! Bloom has thought exactly the same thing about Molly's witticisms (4.519). Husband and wife take a reciprocal interest in each other's minds.

Meanwhile, the sexual drives of men rather disgust Molly—"all the pleasure those men get out of a woman" (583)—but before she knows it she is longing for Boylan again. A train goes by, making her think of men in roasting engines and then of the heat in Gibraltar. The long recollection which follows, the most coherent in the chapter, returns Molly to her youth on the Rock. She remembers her friend Mrs Stanhope and her husband "wogger," and how dull it was after they departed (676). After a digression about love letters (Boylan's "wasnt much"), Molly returns to Gibraltar and Lieutenant Mulvey, the first man to kiss her under the Moorish wall. She told him she was engaged to the son of "Don Miguel de la Flora," a teasing prophecy which came true, thanks to Bloom's last name. In a firtree cove Molly gave the lieutenant pleasure but held herself back a little, pretending not to be excited. Perhaps he married later. Molly remembers their lovemaking with melancholy regret. Like Bloom, she cherishes the "dear deaead days beyondre call" (874) and like him can snap out of senti-mentality. She snaps instantly out of it when she thinks of other female singers, a "lot of squealers." As one would expect, Molly's monologue alludes constantly to vocal music: singers, directions for performance ("chin back," 897), words from songs drawn out in long, melting phrases.

After breaking wind, she feels better, then worries momentarily about Bloom's being led astray by medical students. She cannot get used to his presumption in asking for breakfast in bed. He has always claimed he can do things, such as row a boat (955), always been full of ideas to make a fortune. It was Bloom's idea to send Milly to Mullingar, "on account of me and Boylan," Molly decides. Her daughter is a slyboots, with a sassy tongue. Nearly every observation on Milly's sauciness or prettiness is followed by "like me when I was her age" (1036) or a similar comment. Molly wishes they could have a servant about the house, to make things easier when Bloom brings home friends to entertain. This train of thought is suddenly interrupted when she begins menstruating ("that thing has come on me," 1105). At least Boylan has not made her pregnant, she thinks in consolation as she gets up to use the chamber pot. Memories of a visit to a genteel doctor follow. Molly hopes that in the next world matters will be better arranged for women.

Back in bed, she considers Bloom's good and bad points. He wouldn't have the courage to become involved with a married woman like Josie, but then he doesn't waste money treating his men friends. For most of their male acquaintances Molly feels scant respect, though she remembers with pleasure Simon Dedalus' "delicious glorious voice" and his "flirtyfying" with her (1293). What is his son like? she wonders. The "author" and "university professor" Stephen excites her, and she imagines that his coming into her life was predicted by fortune-telling cards. She will sing for him, perhaps seduce him. Then the young poet will write about her. If that happens, what will Molly do about Boylan? She solves this problem mentally by criticizing "Hugh the ignoramus"; he has "no manners nor no refinement" (1368). The world would be better off if it were governed by women, but a moment later Molly adds that women "are a dreadful lot of bitches." All their troubles make women snappy, and among those troubles is the death of children. Molly contemplates Rudy and the little woolly jacket she buried him in but cuts short her grief.

Her interest in Stephen continues. He could stay in Milly's room, learn Spanish from her, teach her Italian, talk with her.

As for Bloom, she will give him "one more chance," bring him breakfast, and moreover try to arouse his husbandly interest. Bloom has only himself to blame if she's an adulteress; perhaps she will play up to his perversions by charging him money to kiss her bottom (1523). Back to Stephen. Molly plans on cleaning up the house and buying flowers in case Bloom brings the young man back. Flowers make her think of nature, nature of God and the Creation. Foolish men dispute God's existence, whereas "they dont know neither do I so there" (1570). You might as well try to stop the sun from rising as try to dispute that. At this point Molly recalls what Bloom said to her long ago on Howth Head, "the sun shines for you," and we are launched into the rhapsodic memory, or series of memories, which will conclude *Penelope*. Molly's "yeses" come more frequently and her style grows more breathless. She pictures herself and Bloom lying among the rhododendrons and hears him say once again that she is a flower of the mountain. Once again, in memory, she delays her answer to his proposal, looks out over the sea, and thinks of many things— Gibraltar and the watchman going about serene with his lamp and the old castle and the sea crimson like fire and the jessamine and geraniums and how "he," Mulvey, kissed her under the Moorish wall. When she thinks "as well him as another"(1604) she may be remembering what she felt when she gave herself to Mulvey, or what she felt in considering Bloom as husband. "He's" are not sharply differentiated in her mind. But whatever the occasion of her loving may be, the affirmation Molly gives is really to the excitement of loving itself. At the very last, of course, in a mood of mingled ecstasy and resignation, Molly decides to accept Bloom. Prompted by her eyes, he asks his question again, and *Ulysses* ends with her answer.

Afterword

MOLLY SAYS yes. Your comment on reaching the last page of Joyce's novel will depend on the motives you bring to reading it.

Let us say, for the sake of argument, that your motive is the same as Molly's in reading *Ruby: Pride of the Ring* or Bloom's in buying *Sweets of Sin*. It seems highly unlikely that you will be satisfied with *Ulysses* as pornography, though opinion on this point has differed over the years. Like many other early readers Virginia Woolf found the novel at least dirty-minded and vulgar, and the United States Customs Service regarded it as criminally prurient. As a consequence *Ulysses* became the chief exhibit of a celebrated 1933 obscenity trial. Judge John M. Woolsey's decision legalizing the importation of the novel viewed it as "a rather strong draught" with possible "emetic" rather than erotic powers.[1] I would myself argue that *Ulysses* has neither of these biological effects. Obviously, the novel's spoken profanities and obscenities seem much less shocking now than they did to readers in 1922. As for the characters' sexual activity, Molly, say, is frank enough in remembering what she did with Blazes and anticipating what she might do with Stephen, but her frankness about this topic merges with all the other kinds of frankness of which she is capable and becomes part of her full, complicated nature. She is too interesting to be erotic or emetic. The novel does indeed expose pornography to view—"pornographic" seems the only possible word for the lurid lovemaking scene between Molly and Blazes in *Circe*, or for Bloom's excitement at being degraded by "Bello"—but only as part of its study of Bloom's shame-driven imagination. What attracts Joyce's sympathetic interest is the occasional human need for sexual titillation or degradation.

---

1. This decision, amiable and enlightened except for some condescension towards the Irish, is well worth reading; it is printed as a preface to the earlier Random House editions of the novel.

Disappointment, too, seems likely if you read *Ulysses* with Gerty MacDowell's purposes in taking up Miss Cummins' romances *The Lamplighter* or *Mabel Vaughan*—that is, if you read with a heart yearning for a happy ending. In the Joycean scheme of things virtue is not necessarily rewarded, vice punished, or maiden modesty espoused by eligible young men. Some of these events happen, partially; Bloom's generosity to the Dignam family is rewarded to the extent that Martin Cunningham notices it (10.975). Or they do not happen. Or they happen ludicrously:

> A most romantic incident occurred when a handsome young Oxford graduate, noted for his chivalry towards the fair sex, stepped forward and, presenting his visiting card, bankbook and genealogical tree, solicited the hand of the hapless young lady, requesting her to name the day, and was accepted on the spot (12.658).

In this Cyclopean parody Joyce replicates the contrivances and simplifications of romantic fiction. He does much the same with "Matcham's Masterstroke," which Bloom judges to be "quick and neat," also noting that the prize titbit begins and ends morally. Thus Joyce throws into relief the contingencies and complications of his own work. *Ulysses* could not be less quick and neat. Its plot ends with a resounding "and they all lived ever after." For Bloom (as for the original Ulysses) the surviving of a day in order to get to the next represents something of a triumph, but hardly a triumph Miss Cummins would recognize; Molly concedes her husband breakfast in bed while thinking of further occasions to cuckold him. And the other human plots of the novel are just as morally unsatisfying, just as incomplete: Mulligan mocks on with impunity; Stephen has no place to sleep and may or may not return to give Italian lessons; the man in the macintosh wanders into and then out of the story, forever unidentified; J. J. O'Molloy never gets his money; and Gerty limps home alone, dreaming her dreams.

Together with Gerty and the Blooms on the list of readers and their wished-for books we can place Stephen seeking love charms in the eighth and ninth books of Moses, Dilly Dedalus seeking French in Chardenal's primer, and the aged Ann Hathaway seeking pious solace in *Hooks and Eyes for Believers' Breeches*, not to mention such smug readers of their own work as Mulligan with *Everyman His Own Wife* and Father Conmee with *Old Times in the Barony*, a volume of aristocratic history escorting the Jesuit safely out of the present and into times of yore, where he is "humane and honoured"

(10.175). In other words *Ulysses* shows everything about readers' personal needs for love, for self-improvement, for escape, for reassurance. It is an encyclopedia of what the youthful Stephen Dedalus, in a well-known passage of *A Portrait of the Artist*, calls "kinetic" emotions—feelings which compel us in one direction or another. Stephen is holding forth to his friend Lynch:

> The feelings excited by improper art are kinetic, desire or loathing. Desire urges us to possess, to go to something; loathing urges us to abandon, to go from something. These are kinetic emotions. The arts which excite them, pornographical or didactic, are therefore improper arts...your flesh responded to the stimulus of a naked statue but it was, I say, simply a reflex action of the nerves.[1]

Later, in *Ulysses*, Stephen becomes a victim of kinesis himself, but for the moment he is able to generalize calmly, and perhaps a little loftily. For him, Bloom's quite different desires for astronomical knowledge in Sir Robert Ball's *The Story of the Heavens* (the source of his shaky knowledge of "parallax"), and for titillation in James Lovebirch's *Fair Tyrants*, would "simply" be the same reflex of the nerves.

Continuing the explanation to Lynch, Stephen turns to the properly esthetic emotion, which arrests and raises the mind above desire and loathing, which, that is, produces a state of stasis rather than kinesis. After a preliminary definition, he describes the process of esthetic analysis and glosses Thomas Aquinas' important term *consonantia*:

> Beauty expressed by the artist cannot awaken in us an emotion which is kinetic or a sensation which is purely physical. It awakens, or ought to awaken, or induces, or ought to induce, an esthetic stasis, an ideal pity or an ideal terror, a stasis called called forth, prolonged and at last dissolved by what I call the rhythm of beauty.
> ...[Y]ou pass from point to point, led by [the work of art's] formal lines; you apprehend it as balanced part against part within its limits; you feel the rhythm of its structure. In other words the synthesis of immediate perception is followed by the analysis of apprehension. Having first felt that it is *one* thing you feel now that it is a *thing*. You apprehend it as complex, multiple, divisible, separable, made up of its parts, the result of its parts and their sum, harmonious. That is *consonantia*.[2]

---

1. *The Portable James Joyce*, pp. 471–472
2. *The Portable James Joyce*, pp. 472–73, 480.

By "the synthesis of immediate perception" Stephen means the perception of *integritas*, one of the terms (along with *consonantia* and *claritas*) in Aquinas' triune definition of beauty. All this is hardly original. Stephen elucidates matters with the point-by-point clarity of one who has but recently sat through lectures on the history of esthetic philosophy. But it is an important idea to keep in mind, since one motive which is unquestionably rewarded by the reading of *Ulysses* itself is precisely the desire to apprehend "rhythm of beauty." If the young Stephen could read *Ulysses*, he would find it awakening an esthetic stasis rather than an improper kinesis.

In the various dramas of the novel, acted as they usually are by characters filled with desire or loathing, moments of detached esthetic appreciation are rare. We glimpse one in the quietness of Davy Byrne's pub, where Bloom admires the curve of wood in the bar. For the brief moment of his watching, his troubles suspended, he desires not to move forward or backward but holds still, pleased and observant, contemplating a shape. If your reading of *Ulysses* has gone well, you will experience moments of like suspension and pleasure, when you seem to comprehend not just the novel's page-by-page details but the form—"the rhythm of beauty"—of large parts or even of the whole. (Joyce encourages such integrating views by refreshing your memory with summaries, such as the Litany of the Daughters of Erin in *Circe* or the tabulated Bloomian budget in *Ithaca*.) At these moments you keep still, perceiving what it is that holds details of Joyce's novel together in a particular structure, or "pattern" or "shape" or "rhythm" or "harmony": the metaphor used hardly matters. You perceive, for example, all the formal lines Joyce draws between Bloom and Stephen in the early chapters, so as to parallel them, make their mornings part of a single figure. The same Dublin clouds and sun control their shifts of mood; they both remember the pantomime character Turko the Terrible and meditate on human navelcords; they both lack keys; as you have seen, Bloom thinks "We" all by itself on a line in *Aeolus* (7.37) and Stephen thinks "We" all by itself on a line in *Wandering Rocks* (10.878). Everything in this pattern of coincidences encourages you to compare and understand the two characters, of course, but the pattern also gives esthetic satisfaction in itself, merely in the fact of its symmetry, like the complementary paintings of a diptych or the rhyming lines of a couplet.

The patterns of *Ulysses* are shaped of characters and actions, symbols, elements like space and time,[1] phrases (think how often Joyce invokes "love's old sweet song"), and rhetorical strategies. The second chapter exactly balances the next-to-last chapter, both being devoted to questions and answers; in a more general way, chapters full of action but (relatively speaking) linguistically plain, like *Hades* and *Wandering Rocks*, tend to be followed by chapters lacking in action but linguistically elaborate, like *Aeolus* and *Sirens*. Whatever Joyce's medium, his artistry is the same, to play back and forth between likeness and difference, creating regularity, "shape and significance," as Eliot expressed it in his *Dial* review.

By the time you finish *Ulysses* you know that the end of Joyce's fictional day is different from its beginning; things have happened. You know further that this end will lead in the course of a few hours to another morning scene. History will repeat itself from June 16 to June 17, just as it has repeated itself from Greece to Ireland in the Homeric parallels and from Mulvey to Bloom in Molly's amorous recollections. But Joyce will also have convinced you, by the very form of the book, that ends are like beginnings. This is to say that he makes the dominating form of the novel—the one pattern most readers have seen most clearly—a vast circle. *Ulysses* rounds on itself. (Possibly Bloom's liking for a "curve" of wood hints in this direction.) In setting, the end returns us to the house which Bloom left at the start of his day, 7 Eccles Street. In technique, the three opening episodes of the "Telemachiad" match the three closing episodes of the "Nostos." That is, each triad of episodes proceeds from a public scene through a consideration of history to private meditation. With the interior monologue of *Penelope* we recover, after being deprived of it for many pages, the essential technique of all the early chapters. Looking at mere letters, and it is a peculiarly Joycean thing to do to look at mere letters, we observe that Molly's last word ends with the "s" beginning the first word in *Telemachus*.[2] On and on these end-to-beginning correspondences go. For all that *Ulysses* is a novel with an unsettled plot and unresolved issues, it displays as closed and perfected a circular structure as one could wish.

---

1. For an ingenious structural analysis of Ulysses as a series of triads (e.g., *Telemachus* = space, *Nestor* = time, *Proteus* = space/time), see Richard Ellmann, *Ulysses on the Liffey*, pp. 1–26.

2. This anticipates the more elaborate circularity of Joyce's *Finnegans Wake*, where the final words "a last a loved a long the" are completed by the opening words "riverrun, past Eve and Adam's ..."

Let us go back once more to Stephen's theorizing in *A Portrait of the Artist.* If his borrowed notion of *consonantia* does not seem to do justice to the full complexity of *Ulysses,* it may be because the materials of an artistic structure matter as much as the structure itself, and Stephen fails to concern himself with materials. His conceptions are pure, scholastic, abstracted from Dublin. Joyce takes pains to demonstrate the abstraction of his character's conceptions: a smell of wet branches overhead seems "to war against the course of Stephen's thought," he writes, and when a few pages later the young man hears a long dray laden with old iron come rattling and jangling around the corner, he suspends his lecture until it has gone past.[1] What Stephen cannot do, combine esthetics with wet leaves or old iron, Joyce does repeatedly, building up his patterns, circular or otherwise, out of the jumbled objects of Dublin and the casual accidents of life there. He is a sculptor in junk, or what appears to be junk until he has put it into relation with something else. In this he might be said to resemble the Picasso who created a bull's head with horns from an old bicycle seat and handlebars.

All the Modernist writers were devoted to the rhythm of beauty, and all fashioned patterns from materials of a certain consistency and impressiveness—Eliot from the symbols of Christian faith, Yeats from the arcana of Rosicrucianism or the cycles of his private vision, Thomas Mann from Wagnerian myth. Who but Joyce fashioned patterns from the inner organs of beasts and fowls, the sentimental phrases of popular songs, U.P., "Love's Old Sweet Song," Turko the Terrible, casual walks along the strand, Dublin banter, street throwaways, and everything else with which *Ulysses* is crammed? Joyce drops Swinburne's poeticism for the sea, "grey sweet mother," into the opening chapter as preparation for a theme which will culminate in the last chapter, where we view Molly as an elemental force akin to the sea. He works a bit of theatrical slang, "the ghost walks" (= "people are being paid"), into the text of *Aeolus,* where we scarcely notice it, unless we understand that it goes along with the walking ghost in *Hamlet,* the terrifying appearance of his mother's ghost to Stephen, the comical manifestation of Paddy Dignam's ghost to Alf Bergan, the parodied séances of the theosophists ("In the darkness spirit hands were felt to flutter," 12.338), and the ghost story Stephen's pupils want him to tell. No aspect of Dublin life is too trivial to be pressed into artistic service, engaged in a design: when Bloom enters the marital bed at the end of his day, he

1. *The Portable James Joyce,* pp. 473, 476.

removes some crumbs and flakes of potted meat, evidence of Molly's assignation with Blazes. Thus does the obscenity of the much-thought-upon Plumtree's ad finally come home to our hero. The tiny detail also reaches back over hundreds of pages to the crumbs and stains on the carriage seats in the funeral cortège, where they were evidence of ongoing human life in the midst of death, "the most natural thing in the world" (6.108).

Crumbs scattered on a bed hardly seem pertinent to a highly wrought artistic structure, but *Ulysses* is built up of such trivialities and vulgarities, and like all comic masterpieces it draws a particular strength from the clash between ordinary materials and sophisticated treatments. Charlie Chaplin's Little Tramp—a figure more than a little like Leopold Bloom—wears a shabby suit but moves through the city streets, when the occasion demands it, with choreographed grace. Joyce grants Bloom a vision of his dead son at the end of *Circe* and links that vision carefully with the apparition of Stephen's mother earlier in the chapter, thus completing a pattern, but he arranges for Bloom's imagination to costume Rudy in loving bad taste. A comic Joycean wit invents such a moment, just as it invents an ingenious parallel between a Jewish advertising canvasser and the great Ulysses, as it makes a sort of poetry out of potted meat,

> The name on the label is Plumtree. A plumtree in a meatpot, registered trade mark. Beware of imitations. Peatmot. Trumplee. Moutpat. Plamtroo (17.603),

and as it turns casual talk into ordered art. No one could care less about *consonantia* than the foul-mouthed narrator of *Cyclops*, but this narrator's first sentence turns out to be as circularly patterned as *Ulysses* itself. It rounds itself from homonym to homonym, "I" to "eye":

> I was just passing the time of day with old Troy of the D. M. P. at the corner of Arbour hill there and be damned but a bloody sweep came along and he near drove his gear into my eye.[1]

Joyce's magic is always pulling astounding rabbits out of unlikely hats, making you laugh while you wonder how the trick was done.

---

1. "D. M. P." = Dublin Municipal Police. Note how the sentence suggests the Homeric parallel (Ulysses puts out Polyphemus' one eye with his spear), and with "old Troy" perhaps even suggests that it is suggesting the Homeric parallel.

*   *   *

Why should you read *Ulysses?* In pointing out the patterns of the novel, I have given one answer to the question, but I would not wish to rely on this answer exclusively or promote it at the expense of all other possible answers. I have heard some readers of *Ulysses* say that they value it because it so courageously confirms their sense of the moral bleakness of modern life, while others claim that they admire (Stephen's language) its "eternal affirmation of the spirit of man in literature" (17.30). I make no attempt to reconcile these views. It seems to me that little is gained by arguing readers into motives for liking the book, though much may be gained by arguing them away from motives, like a hope for a conventional happy ending, which are bound to make them disappointed. You should read Joyce's novel (or any novel) with whatever motives keep you, no one else, engaged in turning the pages. There are no wrong reasons for reading *Ulysses* with pleasure. Or for reading it with increased pleasure a second time.

Suggestions for Further Reading

THE LIST below is highly selective; I have tried to mention only works potentially useful to relative beginners with Joyce and especially to first-time readers of *Ulysses*. For guidance through the compendious scholarship on the novel, consult the bibliographical essay by Sidney Feshbach and William Herman on pages 754–762 of Zack Bowen and James F. Carens, eds., *A Companion to Joyce Studies* (Westport, CT and London: Greenwood Press, 1984).

Printed materials

Adams, Robert Martin. *James Joyce: Common Sense and Beyond* (New York: Random House, 1966). Though thirty-five years old, this is a good general introduction to Joyce, with an excellent brief summary of Irish history (pp. 3–28) and a solid discussion of *Ulysses* (pp. 117–171).

Adams, Robert Martin. *Surface and Symbol: The Consistency of James Joyce's Ulysses* (New York: Oxford University Press, 1962). Like the previous work, an old book but still an excellent study of Joyce's employment of factual Dublin material in the novel.

Blamires, Harry. *The New Bloomsday Book*, 3rd ed. (London: Routledge, 1996). A lengthy plot summary and commentary, marred somewhat by an insistent theological interpretation of the novel.

Budgen, Frank. *James Joyce and the Making of Ulysses* (London: Grayson & Grayson, 1937). A chatty, old-fashioned book of literary reminiscence by someone who witnessed Joyce's thinking about and work on the novel.

Coyle, John, ed. *Ulysses: A Portrait* (New York: Columbia University Press, 1998). Essays and extracts exemplifying the critical and scholarly responses to the novel since 1922.

Eliot, T. S. "*Ulysses*, Order, and Myth," reprinted as "Myth and Literary Classicism" in *The Modern Tradition*, ed. Richard Ellmann and Charles Feidelson (New York: Oxford University Press, 1965), pp. 679–681. Eliot's famous early review of *Ulysses*, first published in *The Dial* in 1923, which praises Joyce for making a "mythical method" available to modern writers.

Ellmann, Richard. *James Joyce*, new and revised ed. (Oxford and New York: Oxford University Press, 1982). The definitive biography of Joyce and an essential aid. See especially "The Backgrounds of *Ulysses*," pp. 357–379.

Ellmann, Richard. *Ulysses on the Liffey* (New York: Oxford University Press, 1972). Eloquent chapter-by-chapter criticism, particularly interesting for its consideration of an alternate scheme of organization for the novel.

French, Marilyn. *The Book as World: James Joyce's Ulysses* (Cambridge: Harvard University Press, 1976). A conspicuously well-written and interesting general study. Like Schwarz's *Reading Joyce's Ulysses* (see below), this is a good first critical work to consult.

Fuller, David. *James Joyce's Ulysses* (New York: St Martin's, 1992). An accurate and unpretentiously written introduction to the novel; brief summaries of plot events.

Gabler, Hans Walter, with Wolfhard Steppe and Claus Melchior. *Ulysses: A Critical and Synoptic Edition* (New York and London: Garland, 1984). 3 vols. The master text from which the corrected edition of *Ulysses* is printed. If you learn to decipher a set of bibliographical symbols, something which takes time and patience, these volumes will show you how the novel was composed—which sentences were put down first, how they were changed, what was deleted, etc.

Gifford, Don, with Robert J. Seidman. *Ulysses Annotated: Notes for James Joyce's Ulysses* (Berkeley: University of California Press, 1988). The most accurate and encyclopedic guide to the details of the novel, with complete translations of foreign phrases, texts of songs, notes on persons and places, and the like. The excellent index can be used as a concordance to *Ulysses*.

Hart, Clive, and David Hayman, eds. *James Joyce's Ulysses: Critical Essays* (Berkeley and Los Angeles: University of California Press, 1974). Chapter-by-chapter commentaries by various hands; not up to date but reliable and sensible.

Hayman, David. *Ulysses: the Mechanics of Meaning*, rev. ed. (Madison: University of Wisconsin Press, 1982). A short critical study of the novel by a distinguished Joycean. It is not for beginners, perhaps, and is not keyed to the new edition but is otherwise consistently helpful; Hayman's notion of a rhetorical "arranger" as the source of stylistic playfulness in the novel has been influential.

Kenner, Hugh. *Joyce's Voices* (Berkeley: University of California Press, 1978). A witty and subtle short book, mostly on *Ulysses*, by one of Joyce's most sophisticated critics.

Kenner, Hugh. *Ulysses*, rev. ed. (Baltimore: Johns Hopkins University Press, 1987). A more difficult and more compendious study of the novel than *Joyce's Voices*; allusive, probing, and original criticism.

Joyce, James. *Ulysses*, ed. with an introduction and notes by Jeri Johnson (Oxford: Oxford University Press, 1993). This "World's Classics" edition, like the very similar Penguin edition (see below), offers fairly extensive annotation but is based on the old uncorrected text of the novel.

Joyce, James. *Ulysses*, ed. with an introduction and notes by Declan Kiberd (London: Penguin, 1992).

Lawrence, Karen. *The Odyssey of Style in Ulysses* (Princeton: Princeton University Press, 1981). As the title implies, a study of the novel's style, but one which refuses to consider style apart from other aspects of the novel; for example, Lawrence calls *Oxen of the Sun* the chapter Stephen Dedalus would like to have written.

Litz, A. Walton. *The Art of James Joyce* (London: Oxford University Press, 1961). An early, brief, highly perceptive examination of Joyce's revisions to *Ulysses*—these were nearly always expansions, as Litz points out—and what these revisions tell us about the novel.

Maddox, James H., Jr. *Joyce's Ulysses and the Assault upon Character* (New Brunswick: Rutgers University Press, 1978). An excellent chapter-by-chapter examination of Joyce's changing perspectives on the notion of character, which in spite of its title confirms that "character is the closest thing to a constant" in the book.

Norris, Margot, ed. *A Companion to James Joyce's Ulysses* (Boston and New York: Bedford Press, 1999). A critical handbook presenting various approaches to the novel: deconstructionist, psychoanalytical, Marxist, and the like. Most useful for first-time readers is the editor's short "Critical History of *Ulysses*," summarizing responses to the novel over the years.

Raleigh, John Henry. *The Chronicle of Leopold and Molly Bloom: Ulysses as Narrative* (Berkeley: University of California Press, 1977). A painstaking reconstruction of the personal histories of Joyce's main characters.

Schwaber, Paul. *The Cast of Characters: A Reading of Ulysses* (New Haven and London: Yale University Press, 1999). A short critical book by a literary scholar and clinical psychoanalyst.

Schwarz, Daniel R. *Reading Joyce's Ulysses* (New York: St Martin's, 1987). A good first critical book to consult after a reading of the novel; as an interpreter Schwarz is reasonable, lucid, and very well read in Joycean criticism.

Seidel, Michael. *Epic Geography: James Joyce's Ulysses* (Princeton: Princeton University Press, 1976). An exhaustive discussion of Joyce's geographic symbolism, and a detailed comparison, complete with maps, of Bloom's movements about Dublin with Ulysses' movements about the Mediterranean and Ithaca, as the latter were postulated by the French classicist Victor Bérard.

Sherry, Vincent. *Joyce: Ulysses* (Cambridge and New York: Cambridge University Press, 1994). An introduction and a critical interpretation by a prominent Joycean well informed in contemporary literary theory.

Sultan, Stanley. *Ulysses, The Waste Land, and Modernism* (Port Washington, New York, and London: Kennikat Press, 1977). A short and intelligent book about exactly what its title suggests.

Wilson, Edmund. "James Joyce" in *Axel's Castle* (New York: Scribner's, 1931), pp. 191–236. A very early discussion which places *Ulysses* in a literary context and raises still pertinent questions about Joyce's difficulty.

Internet resources

Joycean materials on-line have multiplied astonishingly in recent years and now constitute a major resource for readers, including first-time readers, as long as a due measure of caution and skepticism is brought to the process of using them. As everyone knows, materials are usually posted on the Internet with little or no editorial control; they change (appear, disappear, move sites, get new webmasters) without warning; and are often infuriatingly under construction. Nevertheless they make conveniently available a great range of facts, commentaries, images, academic papers, and discussion groups, and anyone seriously interested in Joyce should at least sample them. Among the most substantial and helpful of Joyce Internet sites are:

The International James Joyce Foundation
www.english.ohio-state.edu/organizations/ijjf

Work in Progress
www.2street.com/joyce

James Joyce Portal
www.robotwisdom.com/jaj/portal.html

James Joyce's Ulysses in Hypermedia
http://publish.uwo.ca/~mgroden/ulysses